Praise for Heart of Relating

This is truly a "Course in Miracles" for relationships.

Malcolm Stern, Co-founder of *"Alternatives"*,
Psychotherapist and Author

Heart of Relating *is a very useful and important work. It gives you, in a concise way, deep insight into how to know yourself and how then to communicate from your essential self to the essential self of others. We are at an epochal time of change in which humanity, worldwide, needs conscious communication skills to be taught and learned as the heart of a secular ethic that empowers all people. This book will give you a jump-start in being a leader in fostering this necessary transformation.*

Richard Moss, MD., Author of *Inside-Out Healing* and *The Mandala of Being*

Every week my work colleagues would ask, "What's the topic?" On "Love Without Falling" Week, I showed them the Love Paradigms Model and they all wanted copies. It touched a chord.

Anonymous member of the first *Heart of Relating* Study Group

I love Heart of Relating - *what a passionate offering to the world. I was inspired to fuse your exercise in "Look Who's Talking" Week with my own work on a teaching weekend and also adapted your wonderful diagram in a workshop for parents. You have clearly articulated what is deeply true and I am sure that your work will be a resource for facilitators to enhance all kinds of self-enquiry workshops.*

Joanna Watters – Teacher and Founder of *This Beautiful Work*:
supporting a radical acceptance of present moment reality

My heart was firmly closed to relationships when I started to use Heart of Relating *to explore my inner world. After only a few weeks, I literally felt my heart opening again and an important, loving relationship fell into this space.*

Elena Brandwood, Occupational Therapist

This is **the** *manual for the nuts and bolts of healthy relating, which should be handed out at birth! I want to see it in every school, church, government, social services department and community of every kind.*

Sally Eaves, Retired School Teacher

The message is pure, simple, easy to grasp and from the heart. As a therapist I will certainly use Heart of Relating *with clients.*

Kat Collier, Massage Therapist

A beautiful blend of deep wisdom and useful strategies for cultivating authentic relationships; most importantly, with ourselves first.

Linda Lantieri, Author of *Building Emotional Intelligence*

On "Ego Watch" Week I made an Egometer, which I put on my car dashboard. This has transformed my driving. I've always enjoyed the thrill of powerful cars, which endangered and scared passengers. The Egometer showed me how often I was speeding and accelerating just to feel better than others. Now I have a smaller car and my Egometer's indicator stays mainly central – meaning that I am calm and non-reactive.

Ian Fenwick, *HR* Study Group Member

Heart
of
Relating

Blessings on all
your relationships

Carmella B Hakl

House of Hahn
Matador
9 Priory Business Park,
Wistow Road
Kibworth Beauchamp
Leicester LE8 0RX, UK
Tel: (+44) 116 279 2299
Fax: (+44) 116 279 2277
Email: books@troubador.co.uk
Web: www.troubador.co.uk/matador

ISBN 978 1784622 923

British Library Cataloguing in Publication Data.
A catalogue record for this book is available from the British Library.

Printed and bound by CPI Group (UK) Ltd, Croydon, CR0 4YY
Typeset by Troubador Publishing Ltd, Leicester, UK

Matador is an imprint of Troubador Publishing Ltd

CARMELLA B'HAHN

Heart
of
Relating

COMMUNICATION BEYOND EGO

Also by Carmella B'Hahn

Benjaya's Gifts (with M'haletta), 1996

Mourning Has Broken, 2002

When I was nine, my headmaster, Mr Partington,
inscribed in my autograph book –

Enquire within upon everything

I did.

This course was crafted for
and is dedicated to
anyone
moved to do likewise –

especially
my son, Asher.

Contents

Finding the Words: My Story

I was speechless as a child for no apparent reason and unable to connect with others or life in a normal fashion. Doctors agreed that I was not autistic, just highly sensitive, and no rational cause was ever found for my silent state. Locked in my inner world, I became an avid people-watcher with a growing fascination for how humans relate. This has never waned.

My first hesitant words tumbled out at six and I remained verbally challenged and petrified of speaking in public for the next 20 years or so. School was difficult – to say the least – and there was no "How to Relate and Communicate" class on the curriculum to assist my progress. Finally, at 29, when speaking live on BBC Television to millions of viewers about the unusual water birth of my son, Benjaya, I realised that at least I had cracked the challenge of speaking to an audience!

So, now I could speak in groups of all sizes, but I was disturbed by communication in general. I was particularly confused by the blatant mismatch between what many people said and what they appeared to be feeling. I longed to discover how to match my inner and outer worlds and how to relate well – especially for my children's sake. I knew that they would imitate my behaviour *and* that *their* natural relating skills held the key to how I wanted to behave around them! They were exquisitely present with everything they encountered; totally authentic without trying.

Sadly, I realised that much of my own intrinsic knowing was in hiding. My teenage desire to look good, be special and be admired had created a mask and I had fallen into emulating others and trying to be someone else rather than allowing my Self to unfurl and express. To create satisfying relationships, I would have drop this mask and set about replacing anything I had absorbed that no longer resonated with me. Replace with what? This was the question that spurred me on to become the hunter/gatherer of the *Heart of Relating* teachings.

It took decades of collection and practice to cover so much ground, but every one of the 52 pieces offered here forms a necessary facet of what I see as the hologram of the art of relating; relating not just to individuals, but to life itself. I succeeded in creating what I needed for myself and it is with delight that I offer these teachings to you as part of my legacy.

A Paradigm Shift in Relating

A revolution in relating is underway across the globe: a paradigm shift in how we relate with all that exists. It is a movement towards relating from our essential Self – the inherent identity that lies beyond our ego. My sincere desire is that the *Heart of Relating* teachings add momentum to this collective wave.

My definition of "paradigm" is:

> *A particular way of viewing, experiencing, valuing and thinking about our reality.*

Human beings enter life with about 100,000,000,000 brain cells, a small proportion of which are wired to oversee our basic bodily functions, but the majority of cells are unwired, awaiting programming from both the societal ways of our time and our particular life circumstances, family beliefs and values.

It is as if we, as youngsters, automatically don the invisible glasses of our culture – which all have a similar lens prescription – and through these lenses we perceive and frame our world. In addition, the colour and depth of tint of our lenses adjusts according to our unfolding personal interactions and life experience. We will continue to wear these metaphoric glasses until the realization dawns that we have been viewing and interacting with life in a prescribed way. When this is brought to consciousness, we can question whether there are changes we feel drawn to make.

Change will, to some degree, happen naturally once we gain insight about what has been clouding our clarity, however, we will need to be pro-active if we want change to last and become embedded in our actions. New habits are born by repetition of action, which grounds our head knowledge – hence the practices in this course.

Heart of Relating focuses specifically on the shift in relating, which includes our relationship with ourself, others and life, but there are paradigm shifts happening in education, medicine, science, technology and other fields.

Quantum leaps in awareness occur when the number of people consistently behaving in new and similar ways reaches a critical mass. The next incoming generation will then accept these predominant ways of being as normal... until the desire for expansion and change is stirred in them.

There is a model at the end of this section that encapsulates what I see as the main components of the two overlapping paradigms of relating at this point in history: the pervading "outside-in" paradigm and the emerging "inside-out" paradigm. This course is designed to assist the migration from the former to the latter, recognising that we are usually in a state of flux and that wherever we are right now is absolutely fine. It supports the truth of Eckhart Tolle's statement,

If you get the inside right, the outside will fall into place.

In a nutshell, the outside-in paradigm of relating is one in which we often feel at the mercy of that which we perceive as being external and separate from ourselves. We communicate mainly from our ego-identity, and failure, fault, blame, right and wrong, good and bad are all a natural part of our mindset and vocabulary.

When we are functioning from the inside-out paradigm, keeping our integrity by staying true to our inner truth is paramount, no matter what is happening externally or what anyone else thinks of us. We perceive and relate from our essential identity beyond our persona; from the aware Self that perceives ego antics. We aspire to "stand with" rather than "separate from" others and life.

Cutting edge research and wisdom teachings agree that the energy *behind* our words – our state of *being* – forms the quality and direction of our lives and relationships. When we are not "at home" with ourselves – not feeling safe – communication tends to go pear-shaped, leaving a mismatch between how we feel inside and the words that leave our lips. *Heart of Relating* helps us recognise when we have drifted off-centre and shows us how to return to the comfort of our home base. It points to what is causing dysfunction and helps create heartful, authentic relationships that embrace challenges as catalysts of awakening. The teachings also help us clean up and match our language to our feelings, and from this aligned place, the many practical skills for effective relating – in these pages or from any other source – have a much higher chance of working.

When embracing the inside-out paradigm, a foundational shift happens as we move from an underlying belief such as this:

Things are not right – I haven't got there yet, but I will make it one day if I keep trying.

To this:

Life is about being present with and opening to what's here now; whatever is presenting itself.

The *Heart of Relating* teachings support the release of striving, seeking and anything that belittles or pushes away any part of ourselves or others. They advocate compassionate acceptance of what's here now and remind us that we will miss what we are looking for if we search for it outside of ourselves.

I, like others who write from this perspective, realize that using words accurately without creating some form of separation is impossible because our language was formed in an "outside-in" paradigm. By Week 51 – Beyond Separation, we will see that even the concept of inside and outside is actually incorrect because the more awareness – or beingness – we experience, the more inseparable inside and outside become. Despite this anomaly, I have chosen to use the inside/outside concept throughout the course because I believe it is a useful stepping-stone to the perception shift that will enrich our relationships and communication.

A new language will develop, of that I am certain; a language that will clarify the difference between the "I" we speak from as ego and persona and the "I" that is a knowing awareness that doesn't exist as a personalised entity. For now, I can only express myself in the language of our time through my own particular lens. You have already noticed, perhaps, that I have chosen to use "Self" when meaning our innate identity and "self" when referring to our persona.

There are countless initiators of this paradigm shift in the field of relating who have informed and inspired me; individuals who have dared to question the status quo and have spent much of their lives discovering alternatives. To them I am extremely grateful, and – believing that inclusivity and networking are vital to the emerging paradigm – where their work expands my own, I have pointed you in their direction.

Now I suggest that you begin by using the model of the two paradigms of relating to see where you stand and where you would like to be – practising self-acceptance if necessary.

The OUTSIDE-IN Paradigm of Relating
I'm on a journey to somewhere else

The world outside my body is separate from me. I conceptualise what I perceive and then relate from my interpretations and opinions *about* it.
How other people perceive me is important. I often morph my behaviour to what I think others want, in order to get approval/results of various kinds.
I engage mainly with the spoken word and what is presented externally, rarely sharing the truth of what I feel inside. There is a mismatch going on.
I relate mostly from and to the human identities (persona) of both others and myself, e.g. appearance, roles, conditioning, status, gender.
My circumstances, history, what others have told me and what I see as my limiting character traits prevent me from fulfilling my dreams.
My ego reacts and my emotional state swings in relation to others and my external world, which I believe is responsible for sending me off-balance.
I imagine I know a lot about others and often pigeonhole them, speak on their behalf, generalise, stereotype, gossip, blame and judge.
On balance, I mostly value: speed, setting goals and making things happen; fixing things and people; the intellect, logic and information.
I am entitled to get my needs met by the world. It's ok to tell white lies, coerce others, and compete to get what I want: there is scarcity out there.
This has gone wrong. Who failed? I deserve to be made to feel bad about this, and to expose and punish those guilty of mistakes or wrongdoings.
I resist, resent, and complain about things that feel uncomfortable and consequently sabotage my natural sense of well-being.

All is in flux, both paradigms merge in us in varying degrees. Neither is wrong.

The INSIDE-OUT Paradigm of Relating
Wherever I am, I'm home

Everything is connected. I experience being *of and with* life and relate using my full body's senses – including feelings, intuition and reason.

Staying true to my own integrity and authenticity is paramount. I notice relationships blossom best when I relate from who *I am…* beyond ego.

I listen and attune to what is going on inside others and myself, behind the words and presenting behaviour. I aim to align my words and feelings.

I relate from an expansive identity that embraces the non-physical Self, i.e. awareness and intuition, and connect to this in others when I can.

I welcome the awareness of what is limiting me and trust that I can find surprising ways to break through. I expand and open to my limitless Self.

I aspire to be in the driving seat of my responses to life's circumstances and know that ultimately I am responsible for my behavior and state of being.

I speak for myself from what I feel to be true in the moment. I am curious and interested in our differences and keen to learn from them.

I value: silence; spaces to just be; feelings; not knowing; sitting with what's not ready to move… until it is; receptivity; insight; *and* intellect/logic etc.

I meet my own needs where possible and clearly and cleanly express them when necessary. I trust that my true needs will be/are being met somehow.

I compassionately accept "failure" and allow it to spur creative change. Every challenge I encounter offers insights about who I am.

I live closely with my inner smile and am grateful for life's rich diversity and the opportunity before me to wake up to greater awareness.

Where do you stand now?   **Model by Carmella B'Hahn**

Choose How to Use

STOP for a moment before leaping into this material. *Heart of Relating* is now yours and you are free to find your best possible method of relating to its contents so that it succeeds in enhancing your relationships and communication patterns for life. You can dip and dive; see what fires or moves you; find your tripwires; talk about topics to all and sundry; use one of the guided structures; read it straight through; or all of the above! Whatever method you choose, I encourage you to engage fully in the practical application of the teachings on the practice pages, to add to what you grasp with your mind from reading the quotes, text and stories. Lasting change requires application of knowledge and insights, to daily living.

Each tree takes exactly a year to form one concentric ring, which is visual evidence of its growth. This is what I am asking you to consider right now.

ARE YOU WILLING TO GIVE YOURSELF THE LUXURY
OF ONE YEAR OF TRANSFORMATIVE PRACTICE
TO SET UP YOUR RELATING SKILLS FOR LIFE?

I know that you won't be alone if you have a barrage of reasons for not taking on one more thing that needs a regular time commitment. We tend to reassess our time priorities only when we get sick or some other circumstance pushes us to the edge. I empathise, and yet I know from experience that telling ourselves and others why we can't find time to do and become what we want to, will serve only to keep us in the exact same position. If we truly want something to occur, there has to come a point when we say, "I choose this as a priority. How can I make it happen?"

There is a choice from two recommended formats if you choose a structured method:

> **Option A – *Heart of Relating* Solo** (Doing the course alone)
> **Option B – *Heart of Relating* Duo or Group**
> (This option is highly recommended for optimal benefit.)

The basic pattern for options A and B is this:

* **Beginning of the week**

Thoroughly read (preferably twice) the four pages of the week's chapter and then do the journal work and preparation exercises from the practice page.

* **During the week**

Follow what you have been asked to do under the practice page subheading, "During the … Week".

* **At the beginning of the following week**

Capture in your journal what had the most impact (and attend your duo or group meeting if taking option B). Then start the next week's lesson as above in "Beginning of the week".

In-depth suggested formats for both options, which guide you how to use the course alone or with others, can be seen at the end of the book. PLEASE VISIT THESE PAGES BEFORE DECIDING how to proceed. Once you start, a simple weekly rhythm will become clear.

You will need:

* A JOURNAL small enough to carry around – A5 size ideal.
* A WEEKLY 45-MINUTE TIME SLOT ALONE

plus 1 – 2 hours weekly if meeting in a duo or group.

* THE COMMITMENT TO KEEP GOING… no matter what.

Bear with me as I impart the rest of the preparation information, all of which I believe is necessary to share after noting the feedback of the pilot study group.

What we each know and practise in our way of relating is unique, and perhaps you are already masterful at some of these teachings. They will almost certainly not all be new to you. You might be knowledgeable *about* some themes and yet could benefit from embodying them further into your way of being, which is where the exercises could be invaluable. Despite having written these exercises, I took part in the pilot *HR* study group and learned a vast amount about my own patterns of relating. I therefore humbly suggest that you practise both the new and familiar teachings to expand and refresh your knowing.

This course is about partaking in a whole, integrated package that needs to cover all the bases to make overall sense. The order of themes was carefully chosen to build a foundation of understanding, so dippers and divers be warned! I recommend you start at the beginning and refer to later topics as required, e.g. "The Heart of Anger" and "Marvellous Mistakes" come later, which could be a crucial support when faced with anger issues or struggling with having made a "mistake". If you peruse the contents pages and scan the chapters in advance, you will have a good idea of the topics covered so that you can jump forward if you need that specific support.

If you are in a partnership or group, you will have to keep to the unfolding order but can personally explore specific topics as needed or wanted and return to these later with others.

If venturing alone on the course, the choice is yours to speed up or slow down the suggested weekly rhythm, *however*, consider that spaciousness is likely to be more effective than speediness. Often a deeper learning will reveal itself when given the space. The pilot feedback made it clear that a week *is* needed per section, and spreading each lesson across two weeks could work even better because more time means more live examples of the topic at hand. Yes, yes, that would take more time in the long run, but this really is a life training!

Humankind tend to approach new ideas by first holding them at a distance, with doubt as the default position:

What if I disagree… or don't understand… or get it wrong… or need to drop my cherished beliefs?

Suggestion: Be like a hungry owl who devours the whole mouse; taking it all in and trusting its wise guidance system to absorb what is needed. Throw yourself in with courage and clear intention and you will be more likely to catch the essence of these rich pickings.

To make things easier to integrate, it is necessary to have some weeks that are more about understanding wider concepts than "solving" and "action". If you are a solution-oriented person you might find yourself asking after certain lessons, "Yes, but what do I *do* with this?" My answer is: be patient and know that grasping a deep concept can be a major step towards a solution presenting itself.

We all have preferred learning styles: visual, hands-on, auditory, conceptual, etc., and this course was created with this in "mind" – taking you into the head, the heart, the intuition, nature, and action. It is designed to stretch your learning modality repertoire, and if you find yourself untouched by a particular practice, you are invited to use your ingenuity and create one for yourself.

After many of the chapters, I have suggested resources to support the theme and take you deeper. Where these are easily accessible – online clips or articles – I strongly suggest you take the time to look at them. Where they are books, you will no doubt want to tune in more carefully as to whether you want to explore the topic further by purchasing material.

We all have wounds and it is inevitable that some of you will be triggered by certain themes and practices. Please seek professional support if you need it. Relationships can send us to deeply painful places, but I particularly like this quote:

> *Relationships are the crucible for awakening.*
> ~ ROBERT AUGUSTUS MASTERS
> (Author/Relationships Expert)

(A crucible is defined as a container in which substances are subjected to a high temperature, or as a difficult trial in which elements interact, leading to the creation of something new.)

Now, I have one last thing to put to you before you move on. The revolution in relating, that I mentioned earlier, is happening because people like you are craving more healthful and effective ways of relating. If these teachings work for you, if they inspire you, will you support my dream and spread the word as far and wide as possible? Would you be willing and able to join those generous readers who are buying one or more extra copies of *Heart of Relating* to give as a gift to others who could make an important difference by embracing and sharing this course? I dream of partners, families, students, teachers, therapists, group members, business people, leaders, healthcare workers, church and community members, all learning to relate together, with heart.

For more about the "Buy One, Set One Free" campaign
see: www.heartofrelating.com/books/heart-of-relating

We do not grow absolutely, chronologically.
We grow sometimes in one dimension,
and not in another; unevenly.
We grow partially. We are relative.
We are mature in one realm, childish in another.
The past, present, and future mingle
and pull us backward, forward,
or fix us in the present.
We are made up of layers, cells, constellations.

~ ANAÏS NIN
(Novelist)

The Temptation[1]

Humans learn like this:
(Apply model to learning to ride a bike)

Step 1. Unconsciously Unskilled
"Is there something to learn?"

*Step 2. Consciously Unskilled
"Wow – I have a lot to learn!"

Step 3. Consciously Skilled
"Look at me, I can do this now!"

Step 4. Unconsciously Skilled
"Done that. What's next?"

The skill is now automatic and integrated, and
new neural pathways have been made in the brain.

Friendly Warning!
*Step 2 holds the temptation to give up.
This is where we usually feel out of our comfort zone
and want to retreat
to the safety of familiar habits.
Stay with this step and the rewards will flow.

The
Weekly
Teachings

WEEK 1

Awakening the Body

Listening to our bodily senses

* Opportunity *

To feel more alive and in direct rapport with
others by employing a whole range of bodily
senses when relating.

*Most people don't inhabit a living reality
but a conceptualized one.*

~ ECKHART TOLLE
(Author and Consciousness Teacher)

TIP FROM HR STUDY GROUP
*Write or type out each week's key focus or practice questions
and stick them somewhere visible to jog your memory.
Post-its are great for this.*

Wе have bodies that can touch, feel, taste, smell, hear, see and intuit. As youngsters, unless stifled, we instinctively engaged these luscious faculties with gusto, staying with each encounter until satiated – grabbing a finger, earth in the mouth, stamping in puddles, watching insects, howling in discomfort, inhaling mama's smell, knowing our hunger, sleeping when tired, etc. What happened? How come so much of adults' relating is head-led and disembodied? Experiencing our bodily senses directly is fundamental to successful relating and is a beneficial place to begin.

Spoken words are invaluable in helping us gain rapport and greater understanding of each other, however, they can trap us in the mental realm and create distance. Naming everything is useful and yet can give us a false sense of knowing what we've named, e.g. "That's an oak tree" can stop us from sitting *with it* to sense its presence.

The same is true of labelling humans. When my hair went silver, I noticed young people looking straight through me as they hadn't before, as if their mental labelling scanner was saying, "Older person... not of interest to me". This "categorise and dismiss" behaviour is an example of outside-in relating. Inside-out relaters are more open; they know everything is connected and use bodily cues, including intuition, to sense which connections to follow.

DO WE COMMUNICATE FROM A STANCE OF SEPARATION –
OBJECTIFYING AND SHARING OPINIONS *ABOUT LIFE,*
OR FROM A SENSE OF *BEING WITH* LIFE?

This shift from the head (thinking about) back to our natural, open childlike way of relating (being with) needs us to discern the difference between thinking and awareness. The challenge, which we will visit from various angles, is to allow ourselves to drop into deeper awareness and to learn to use our amazing thinking process consciously in conjunction with this awareness. Relationships with all and sundry – including this course – will improve dramatically once we engage our bodily senses and loosen any notion that we *are* our thoughts and intellect.

* Story Time *

All that Matters is Love
Abigail Robinson[2]

My strongest memories of my grandmother are of her in a Vitesse sports car with red leather seats and a polished wood dashboard, her white hair flowing stylishly out of her headscarf and dark glasses adding to the exuberance and outrageousness. Those days, full of vodka, speeding fines and an abundance of chocolates, were long before Alzheimer's tempered her soul.

When I visited her at the nursing home, where at ninety-nine she became a resident, I was saddened and disturbed by this transition. She was too far away to reach with just words. Absent and unmoving in her chair, only love would pull her back, would allow her to meet my gaze as I crouched in front of her.

I had learned from my work as a healer to gather myself into a fully embodied presence, which means surveying all of my thoughts and feelings, however difficult, and, if necessary, including any sensations of numbness. When I witness all of myself and my sensory experiences, I can ensure no part of me is an obstacle to being an open conduit for love.

Puzzled my grandmother would say: "I don't know you!" and I would reply, "It doesn't matter who I am, all that matters is that I LOVE YOU!" On some occasions our conversation had to be shouted above the exaggerated drama of loud soap operas and in front of staff and residents:

> I don't know why I am SO OLD and STILL ALIVE!
> *You are DYING, piece by piece, A LITTLE BIT AT A TIME.*
> IT'S DIFFICULT DYING!
> *...It's DIFFICULT LIVING!*
> I don't remember anything!
> *You don't need to remember anything. All that matters is that I LOVE YOU!*

One day, soon after I had spoken again about love, thoughtfully and slowly, my grandmother looked at me as if feeling its truth fully for the first time and said:

> Somebody once told me that there is one thing that IS important to remember:
> ALL... THAT... MATTERS... IS... LOVE!

✳ The Practice ✳

Awakening the Body

You will need your journal now and at the beginning of each week's practice.

Awakening the Senses Exercise

Do this in nature or inside. Find a *small* area that catches your eye – around a tree or flowerbed, bookshelf, fruit bowl etc. Now carefully observe, name and describe to yourself in detail what you can see.

Next, put on a blindfold or close your eyes and employ all your other senses. Spend about five minutes touching, feeling the textures, listening, tasting if appropriate, smelling, and sensing the essence of the subject of your attention. Keep releasing *thought about* and sinking into *being with* and experiencing your chosen focus.

Use your journal to catch what touched you in this exercise and note how this could relate to your communication.

During "Awakening the Body" Week

See how often you can catch yourself lost in thought *about* something – maybe categorizing and dismissing someone/thing. Congratulate yourself for noticing and open to what your body might have to say:

- What are my body senses telling me about this and is there a constructive action I could take in response to what it's saying?

For example: You are having a dinner party and a guest begins describing in graphic detail an encounter he had with a sharp knife. You have a thing about sharp knives and realise you are wincing and your appetite is diminishing. Your body is saying, "NO, STOP! This isn't nourishing." You can suffer in silence or employ another option such as honouring your body's message by asking the guest to change the subject.

Note what has had impact on you this week and how you will apply it.

Supportive Resources: David Abram[3] and Thomas Huebl teachings[4]
How Schools Kill Creativity, TED Talks video, Sir Ken Robinson.[5]

WEEK 2

Oh Yes I Can!

Releasing limitations

---

* Opportunity *

To perceive the limitations of "I can't" and to
recognise new realms of possibility.

Nothing is impossible,
the word itself says, "I'm possible"!

~ AUDREY HEPBURN
(Actress)

PLEASE NOTE

This week is about becoming conscious of and choosing to step out
of limitations that don't serve us, where we can.
It is not about denying our feelings and difficulties.

"I can..." opens doors to what we want and has an optimistic flow about it. The words arise from a place of openness and possibility inside us, no matter what others think. **"I can't..."** or "It's just the way I am!" closes doors, seals our apparent limitations and leaves no path to solutions. It is rarely true and often what an outside voice has told us. Whenever we use it – I can't make myself heard; I can't keep my mouth shut; I can't speak in groups; I can't apologise; I can't make new friends etc., these two powerful words prevent progress.

This lesson is right near the beginning so that whenever "I can't..." raises its shaking head to anything suggested, there is every reason to rehearse an alternative response and to open to success. What we are afraid of facing and learning are places of potential breakthrough.

By the way, "I'll try", "I'll attempt to" and "I'd like to" are not alternatives that are likely to work. Imagine your mind is the computer, the keys are at your fingertips, and you operate the "try", "attempt to" and "like to" commands.

Alternatives to "I can't" that have a better chance
- Oh yes I can!
- I choose to make a first step...
- I dare to...
- I haven't learned to do that... yet.
- Will you help me with...?
- What I mean is, I am choosing not to until...

("I can't" is often used as an excuse when we don't want to.)

What we claim we can't do or be can become a comfortable and familiar part of a limited identity. Telling others of our inadequacy and smallness can be used as an indirect and ultimately unfulfilling way to get attention, sympathy or a rescue response from others. The "I can't cook!" mantra could entice sympathetic mothering behaviour from others who then cook for us, thus supporting our limitation by depriving us of the impetus to learn a useful life skill.

> IF WE TRULY WANT TO ACCOMPLISH SOMETHING,
> WHY NOT GIVE IT OUR ALL AND OPEN TO HELP?

Story Time *

The Birth of a Voice

"I can't speak" was my daily mantra until one pivotal moment when I dared to commit to giving verbal communication everything I'd got.

The following story is told by my mother, M'haletta, and is taken from *Benjaya's Gifts,*[6] my first book, which was co-written with her. I was known as "Virginia" then.

She has been at school a year now and as far as I know talks to no one, not even answering a polite "yes" when the teacher calls the register. I do not understand, and neither I think does she. Sometimes she tries to say something and her voice is a croak, sounds are strangled, tears fall again and again – frustration, embarrassment, despair. She seems to have the expectation that we should all be able to read her mind and respond to her needs without words – but we cannot.

It is September. She has moved to another class where the vicar's wife is teaching. There is no difference, though she hears everything and lessons are perfectly produced on the page.

The Christmas Nativity play is being cast and Virginia ventures to put up her hand to play the Virgin Mary. The vicar's wife, with inspired wisdom, supports this shocking, silent request. Virginia brings home the script and studies it quietly. It is to be performed to all the parents, and there is an understudy primed. If ever a choice had been made to hold an audience captive, then this is it. The parents all know her and have shown a puzzled compassion in their concern for her disability.

She enters confidently on Joseph's arm and then she speaks:

"I have travelled a long and weary road…"

Every word rings with crystal clarity. There is silent amazement. No one breaks the spell of her sound.

* The Practice *

Oh Yes I Can!

Exercises

1. Say aloud, "I can't" and let your body freely express the energy of your words. Note your tone of voice, body stance and feelings as you do this. Do the same while saying aloud, "I can" and notice the difference. Repeat this with a partner, if you can, and witness each other. This can be done in your *HR* Study Group if you have one.

2. Hold a small unbreakable object – like a pen – very tightly in front of you. Tell yourself, "Try and drop it" and see what happens.
Hold it tightly again and say, "I allow it to drop now".
Capture the results of both exercises in your journal and talk about any learning with others.

During "Oh Yes I Can!" Week

1. Notice how many times you and others close the door to forward movement by saying, "I can't…" or other limiting statements. Test out the previously listed alternatives on your own "I can'ts".
Catch in your journal what you sensed worked and didn't.

2. The Magic Yet Practice

Play with the magic "yet" word. If you find yourself making a limited statement that you don't want to be true, see how you can use "yet" to leave an opening for change, e.g.:
- I haven't learned this very well… *yet*   • I can't cook… *yet*
- I can't speak about this calmly… *yet*

The yet practice will help you through step 2 (Consciously Unskilled) of the Temptation Model.

3. Observe what "I can'ts" you find yourself wanting to hold onto (the stuck places), and give attention to what you gain from holding on. No need to change anything, just allow awareness to arise and write about it in your journal. Change usually happens of its own accord when the unwanted behaviour is brought to consciousness.

Be clear about what has had impact and how you will apply it.

WEEK 3

Look Who's Talking

Expanding the identity from which we relate

> ### * Opportunity *
>
> To question and expand our identity to
> include both the physical and
> non-physical aspects.

After an extraordinary near death experience:[7]

In that state of clarity, I also realised that
I am not who I thought I was:
Here I am without my body, race, culture, religion or beliefs…
yet I continue to exist!
Then what am I? Who am I?
I certainly don't feel reduced or smaller in any way.
On the contrary,
I have never felt so huge,
this powerful,
or this all-encompassing.

~ ANITA MOORJANI
(Author and Teacher)

Our sense of who we are – our identity – is the springboard for every word we utter. If asked, "What is your identity?", most of us would describe aspects of ourselves from the "Human Identity" circle below. After all, we show up as unique, physical beings.

But what if this human identity is an essential, temporary, part-expression of who we are – our focus for physical life experience – *and* we have a non-physical identity that is a wise witness to the action of our physical life? What if this non-physical Self *is* our intrinsic, intelligent awareness that resonates with truth; an identity beyond beliefs, roles, opinions, conditioning, etc.? What if we were born with pure awareness and have accrued, over time, layers of persona (or ego) that hide this expansive core? This is what wisdom teachers throughout time have told us is so. The original purpose of meditation and all spiritual practice was surely to discover this state of Self and include it in daily living as much as we are able?

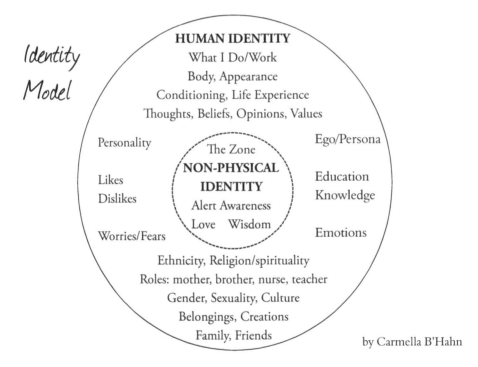

Identity Model

HUMAN IDENTITY
What I Do/Work
Body, Appearance
Conditioning, Life Experience
Thoughts, Beliefs, Opinions, Values

Personality

Likes
Dislikes

Worries/Fears

The Zone
NON-PHYSICAL
IDENTITY
Alert Awareness
Love   Wisdom

Ego/Persona

Education
Knowledge

Emotions

Ethnicity, Religion/spirituality
Roles: mother, brother, nurse, teacher
Gender, Sexuality, Culture
Belongings, Creations
Family, Friends

by Carmella B'Hahn

TO RELATE FROM THE INSIDE-OUT WE NEED
TO GET WISE TO THE SOURCE OF OUR EXPRESSION

Tell Me Who You Are

The harmony singers drifted homeward,
leaving two of us
basking by the deep red fire.

"Tell me who you are," he asked of me,
"if you are not too tired."

"I have many 'I's," said one of them,
"which would you like to meet?"

"The embodied wise one," he replied,
without missing a single beat.

Smiling, I reached for his hand
and we sat in warm silence,
out of our minds,
sharing a harmony without words.

~ CARMELLA B'HAHN

✳ The Practice ✳

Look Who's Talking

This week we will explore the extent to which we are attached and relate from what I am calling our "human identity". The exercise is about becoming conscious of the aspects that make up what most of us mean when we say "me" or "I". Next week (In the Zone) covers our "non-physical identity" and how we can more readily access it.

Exercise: Who am I without…?
Sit and look at the Human Identity circle of the Identity Model and ponder on the particular combination that makes up your persona. Now imagine that each of these aspects of you are removable, like layers of clothing, and visualise taking off as many layers as you can to find out what's underneath them. Each time you remove something, ask:

 ◆ **Who am I without…?**
 (my job, appearance, belongings, etc.)

Be curious if you find yourself resisting removing something and notice the things you feel lighter without. Make journal notes about anything arising from this exercise. Continue to play during the week with the concept of taking aspects of your human identity on and off.

During "Look Who's Talking" Week
Contemplate and discuss this quote by St. Francis of Assisi:
> *What we are looking for is what is looking.*

Notice how much you think, communicate and act on automatic pilot from your human identity – or persona – as if that is *all* you are. Remind yourself of your innate wise witness. The you that is looking, holds a calm, wider perspective and has little interest in getting hooked into life's dramas. Practise relaxing into simply being and watching with interest while apparent difficulties unfold around you.

At the end of the week, write in your journal about any ways that your sense of identity has changed (if any) and ask yourself what you want to remember, and maybe activate, from this week's lesson.

Recitation
Practice

A question was introduced in the last section
that is absolutely key to this course, i.e.:

Who and what is the "I" from which I am relating?

This central theme is reinforced at intervals
between the weekly teachings by a series of statements
taken from *The Pocket Ken Wilber*.[8]

I echo the suggestion Wilber makes to his readers:
Silently recite these statements slowly to yourself,
realising as vividly as possible
the import of each statement.

Recitation Practice

*I have a body
but I am not my body.*

*I can see and feel my body,
and what can be seen and felt
is not the true Seer.*

*My body may be tired or excited, sick or
healthy, heavy or light, but that has
nothing to do with my inward I.*

I have a body but I am not my body.

~ KEN WILBER

WEEK 4

In the Zone

Finding our core

> ## * Opportunity *
>
> To use the immense resources we have to
> assist us back into our core
> when we are out of alignment.

*The ability to be in the present moment
is a major component
of mental wellness.*

~ ABRAHAM MASLOW
(Psychologist)

The Zone is the resulting experience when "thinking *about*" has ceased and when we have surrendered any need for control over anyone or any aspect of our life. When we are in the Zone, we are in alert awareness and feel present with whoever and whatever is before us, which could be described as the aligned experience of our non-physical identity expressing through our human identity. Relating from the Zone flows, as if words and actions *arise* rather than being thought up, sometimes leaving us surprised.

Here are some words to represent the Zone, offered by participants of a Conscious Communication workshop

Presence ~ Juicy aliveness ~ The now ~ Heart space ~ Alert ~ Resonant ~ Awareness ~ Real ~ Limitless ~ Natural ~ Expanded ~ Whole ~ In tune ~ Love ~ Centred ~ Source ~ Beyond thought ~ Just being ~ Infinite potential ~ Core ~ Consciousness

Despite these positive sounding words, all kinds of feelings arise in the Zone, including both pain and bliss. Whatever we experience, it touches us deeply and can have the magnetic effect of causing others to fall into the flow like a slip-steam. Naked experience is attractive.

We have numerous ways of entering this natural state of being, or at least starting the spiral towards it… and often it happens by itself.

Ways that help many of us enter the Zone

Connect with nature ~ Be alert to each moment ~ Be Silent ~ Exercise in a way we love ~ Dance ~ Play inspirational music ~ Sing or make sounds ~ Watch a candle or fire burn ~ Play with a young child ~ Meditate ~ Garden ~ Cook something delicious ~ Make love ~ Be with animals ~ Express love ~ Be still

IT DOESN'T MATTER
THAT WE FALL OUT OF THE ZONE…WE WILL!
WHAT MATTERS IS THAT WE LEARN TO GET BACK IN.

Each week, *Heart of Relating* will bring awareness to the ways we stray from the Zone and will encourage us back in… repeatedly.

* Story Time *

Running into Wisdom

Once, I had a client who was crumpled with distress about another failed relationship and was weeping his way through my tissue supply. The more he focussed on what had gone wrong, on who said what and how badly he'd failed, the more he felt it… again. He could see only the limitations of his personality – nothing more. Childhood pain rose up and a reservoir of his lifetime's grief spilled out.

As counsellor, my job is to listen, witness, and then, if possible, support the client's movement towards the Zone where their own inner resources and answers are accessible. And so, I listened with compassion, noting his relief at simply being heard without blame. He could have gone on…and on… making more and more connections to places of pain, but when the sobs had subsided somewhat, I gently intervened with a question:

"Would you tell me what makes you forget yourself and causes your heart
to sing?"

He sat bolt upright instantly, put down the tissues, and smiled (it was that easy). "Running along green lanes," he said. He then animatedly described how he feels a connection to something greater than himself and how inspiring ideas flood in when running.

So, now that he had been heard and accepted in his crumpledness, he decided it would be a brilliant idea to go running in the lanes simply holding (not actively thinking up answers to) two questions: What can I learn from this relationship challenge? How else could I relate to "failure"?

He brought his pain constructively to the Zone where he did receive insight. Later, he spoke of what stopped him from taking this route of stepping into a different space:

"The challenge for me lies in *choosing* this option when feeling swamped
by distress that seems to crave sympathy. I realise that sometimes I think
I'm asking for help but I just want to retell the story to get someone on
my side. This pattern keeps me stuck."

✳ *The Practice* ✳

In The Zone

Brainstorm in your journal ways that you reach, or have reached, the Zone. Remember specific times when you felt the most at home in your skin at the same time as feeling aligned with something more expansive than your everyday self. Re-visit the most powerful memories and notice how you feel in your body as you remember. You might not be able to recreate these actual experiences, but a memory can influence your present state as if it were happening now.

Choose one memory that will act as an inspiring resource when you need it – especially this practice week, e.g. I felt total relaxation when I allowed the ocean to support me. Make your memory vivid, embellish it if you like, and notice your feelings and the position of your body. Are there key words that come to you that match this memory, such as "I am held"?

During "The Zone" Week

When triggered off balance, take note of the first feeling reaction in your body, e.g. knot in my stomach, queasy, and felt flustered when s/he said "…". Now you are conscious of this feeling reaction, you can use it as a signal, a "choice-point" to call you back to the Zone.

At any hint of a similar off-centre reaction, decide if you want to change your trajectory… or not. If you do, focus instantly on your chosen memory and bring it alive. Say key words if you have them. (If this is tricky on the spot, go into a different room/place as soon as you can.) If you have more time, do anything that is practically feasible from your brainstorm, e.g. running or being with an animal.

Keep at it, experiment with stepping into the Zone and your communication *will* improve by itself. Remember, this is not an avoidance strategy. When you are in the Zone, an inspired response is more likely to be forthcoming. Simply holding the intention to speak from a more spacious Zone-like place can transform a conversation.

As usual, note what you intend to apply from this week's learning.

Watching the Match

Aligning with the unspoken

* Opportunity *

To cultivate a fuller awareness and
understanding of the meaning of the
unspoken that accompanies spoken words.

*The most important thing in communication
is hearing what isn't said.*

~ PETER F. DRUCKER
(Management Consultant)

TIP FROM HR STUDY GROUP

*If you like to learn by verbal exchange rather than writing,
plan to do the course this way. Keep talking about the
content as well as applying the learning.*

Outstanding communicators watch the match of the inner world and the outer expression and have learned to read non-verbal cues that silently speak volumes. Words are wondrous tools for expression but, like puppets on strings, they are animated by what lies *behind* them. Focussing on words alone can tie us in knots. Have you ever been accused of saying something you didn't say, and you've denied saying it, knowing full well that you *did* think and feel it?

Imagine this scene:

Do you like my dress for Suzie's wedding? (With a furrowed brow and biting on a fingernail – hoping for approval.)
It's lovely, nice colour. (After a hesitant silence, with placating tone and one eye still on the TV.)
You don't like it do you? (She knows he's not impressed.)
That's not what I said! (But it is what he thought.)

He might have had a different response had he muted the TV and swivelled towards her with a kind smile saying, "You're nervous I won't like it aren't you? What matters to me is that *you* like it."

If someone verbalises one thing and their non-verbal signs say something else, it will be the non-verbals that hold the key to the full picture. It is difficult for the body to lie, and any mismatch will inform us that the whole story is not on the table. Once we realise a piece of the story is missing, we can ask for more information if it feels right to do so, or gracefully let it go.

CAN WE UTILISE OUR EYES
AND OUR FULL BODY "FEELING ANTENNAE"
TO HEAR WHAT ISN'T SPOKEN?

The awakening the body theme is being expanded here and will continue to arise. *Heart of Relating* will remind us frequently to listen to *all* the cues and to express the numerous parts of ourselves truthfully so that our body language and all our senses and feelings naturally match what comes out of our mouths.

Less than Half the Story

Words are less than half the story:
The spoken tip of our truth.

Listen to silence, distance and space,
intention, tone, and the look on a face.
Notice the eye contact, gestures,
and the way that they lean.
These things speak volumes
about what we all mean.

And what of heart, wisdom and attitude?
What of juiciness, self-worth, humour and gratitude?
And the part of our ego
that is sure
it knows
and the feeling world
in which everything flows.

These are some of the parts
that join the words
that make up the whole
of the story.

~ CARMELLA B'HAHN

* The Practice *

Watching the Match

Start a **Non-verbals** page in your journal. Write the following title words (and/or others) with quite a bit of space around them:

Uninterested   Fascinated   Urgent to speak   Busy

One by one, vividly remember or imagine yourself being in each of these states when someone was/is speaking to you, and identify the non-verbal bodily and behavioural cues you display in this situation.
Write your felt responses in the space around the words, e.g.

eyes glazing and lost eye contact

tiny sighs   **UNINTERESTED**   fidgeting

strategising how to respond and not listening

During "Watching the Match" Week
1. When *others* are speaking to you, notice any non-verbal reactions in yourself and keep your awareness tuned for other things that go on in your body that you might have missed in the journal exercise. Be alert to your feelings, facial expressions, eye contact, breathing, body posture, distance from the speaker, hand/feet movement and physical comfort. At the end of the week answer in your journal:
  • To what extent do my words match my feelings?

2. When *you* are speaking, practise "reading" the responses of your listener(s). Use your eyes, gut reaction and intuitive senses to gauge their non-verbal responses. Your communication will certainly improve if you take these signals into account as you speak as well as checking out your guesses, e.g. "Are you too tired to take this in?"

3. Watch out during any electronic communication in which you cannot see or hear the other. It is severely limited by the absence of non-verbal cues. You will need to be more specific for clarity.

Use your journal to catch insights/changes you choose to make and perhaps highlight or write in capitals any clear action steps.

WEEK 6
Inner Talk

Transforming the critical voices

---

* Opportunity *

To increase self-esteem and health by
releasing critical self-talk and creating a
sound sense of worth from which to relate.

Change cannot be sustained,
unless the individual has the self-worthiness
to accept the potential benefits
gained from the change.

~ MARIO MARTINEZ
(Clinical Neuropsychologist)

PLEASE NOTE

The "Who Said That?" chapter (Week 20) expands this theme
to include inner voices that appear not to be our own.

Remembering to relate as much as we can from our non-physical, expanded Self offers a shortcut to successful relationships, however, some of us suffer from low self-esteem and often feel pulled to identify with what we perceive as our human limitations. A negative self-image can block us from operating from alert awareness – from wisdom. It is therefore important to accept, nurture and celebrate the miracle of our unique human beingness, no matter what its quirks.

Do we look into our eyes in the mirror and soften with tenderness, as if seeing an old friend we love, or do we criticise the external shell we call "me" and forget the whole being that lies behind the image? Next to my bathroom mirror is a quote by the mystic, Kabir, saying:

But if a mirror ever makes you sad,
you should know that it does not know you.

How well do we know the essence, the flavour, of who we are? Widespread "outside-in" conditioning tells us that worth is earned by doing and being good and that seeking the approval of others is the way to bolster it. Putting our own needs last and voicing our shortcomings are generally seen as virtuous, and singing our own praises as egotistical. Perhaps it is time to re-reclaim the exquisite worth with which each of us entered this world.

OUR MOST IMPORTANT RELATIONSHIP IS WITH OURSELF.

Our relationship with self and others will transform once we catch and change our critical self-talk. Starting NOW, we can create a new inner voice that has the power to raise our self-esteem, revitalise our mood, release stress and prevent illness.

Steps to Transforming Critical Self-talk
   1. Get conscious and specific about ways I put myself down.
   2. Ask: Is this thought/comment true or useful in any way?
   3. Separate what I did or didn't do, from my worth.
   (Am I upset by who I *am*, or by what I *did*?)
   4. Ask: What would I like to hear from myself right now?
   5. Look for the learning/the gift and possible action.

Voicing Change

Again those voices play in my head;
heavy-weight words that hang like lead.
They pose as "me", criticise and cajole,
but whose words are these and what is their role?
Let me listen to them without the urge to contract.
Let me know that I have the right to speak back.

They tell me I'm stupid when I make a mistake,
that my memory for names is a total disgrace.
They moan that I'm over the hill – in physical decline,
and a failure with numbers, as if it's a crime.
Wherever they come from, whatever they say,
do I trust these voices, now… today?

Come to think of it, NO!
And about the statements above -
not one of them holds a morsel of love.

~ CARMELLA B'HAHN

* The Practice *

Inner Talk

Start an "Inner Talk" page in your journal. Brainstorm any critical self-talk statements that you use often and write them in speech bubbles. Here are a few examples:

I'm such an idiot; I can't believe I did that!; I'm unattractive; I'm hopeless at sport; I can't make friends; I never get it right; I am failing as a parent; I'm not popular; I'll never pass this exam; I'm a fraud.

"My body is unacceptable"

Taking one speech bubble at a time, apply the five "Steps to Transforming Critical Self-talk" (listed previously) to create ideas for constructive self-talk to practice during the week, e.g.:

1. I'm telling myself I am an idiot and feeling bad.

2. Untrue and not useful. Spilling coffee doesn't make me an idiot.

3. My lapse of concentration is nothing to do with my worth.

4. It's a shame about the lost coffee, but well done for moving quickly and protecting the computer.

5. I will now make a place where I can safely put my drinks.

During "Inner Talk" Week

1. Keep your journal with you and note any other critical self-talk that arises. Aim to bring in a kinder tone and supportive words when you catch that part that's putting you down. Apply the "Transforming Critical Self-talk" steps on the spot if you can and catch the results in your journal as soon as you have time.

2. Absorb all appreciation or compliments as fully as possible.

3. Singing Your Own Praises

If you have an *HR* partner or group, do the following exercise together, otherwise, find someone who is willing to do this with you. Take five minutes each to talk about all the things that you like most about yourselves and anything you have done that you are proud of. Encourage each other to keep going if need be, then talk about the experience and make notes.

What insights from this week will you apply to your everyday living?

Ego Watch

Identifying ego antics

---

* Opportunity *

To learn to recognise the antics of ego and
to free ourselves from the complication it
creates in communication.

---

*The stronger the ego,
the stronger the sense of
separateness between people...*

*The end of ego is the disidentification
of consciousness from form.*

~ ECKHART TOLLE
(Author and Consciousness Teacher)

PLEASE NOTE

*You will need a little longer this week
in order to make your Egometer.*

The ego is said to be a necessary part of human development – a constructed sense of individual self or persona, from which to operate and navigate life. So, egos are not intrinsically bad, but they do have an unfortunate habit of running away with themselves and tricking us into believing that they are our identity – all of who we are.

The ego's need to continually affirm its existence and be our master, rather than servant, severely taints and confuses our relationships. It bends over backwards to be seen as special and different, and one thing the ego loves is comparison. It compares and makes itself better or worse than others, often see-sawing from one to the other. "Better than" puffs us up with a false sense of self-importance and superiority. "Worse than" also gives reason to be different because we've got more or worse problems than most… are more inadequate.

Worse than:
- I feel stupid because my mind isn't sharp like his.
- Your communication puts mine to shame.
- I feel like a blob standing next to her!

Better than:
- What *is* she wearing? I wouldn't be seen dead in that!
- I'll show him not to drive so slowly… overtake… zooooooom!
- This is basic common sense. I can't believe you don't do it.

When we judge ourselves as "worse than" we can be quieter, deflated, withdrawn, miserable, complaining. When considering ourselves "better than" we might become louder, angry, impatient and patronising with a self-righteous tone. We each have our own unique style, be it blatant, subtle, or somewhere in-between.

> THE EGO'S FEAR OF NON-EXISTENCE (DEATH)
> IS THE REASON FOR MOST OF OUR
> DYSFUNCTIONAL COMMUNICATION HABITS.

Discovering, releasing and replacing the habitual patterns that have become like an overcoat to our real selves (like many of the things in the Human Identity circle) is a practice that will continue throughout.

Making an Egometer

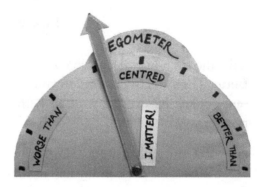

You will need: Coloured card or cereal box, small side plate, compass (optional), pencil, eraser, pen, scissors, paper glue, ruler, a split pin paper fastener *or* a drawing/map pin and piece of Blu-tack. (If you don't have a paper fastener – the best option for making the pointer swivel – use a pin until you can get to a stationer. Share one box of these if in a group.)

Refer to the pictures as you follow instructions:

1. Cut out a circle of card by drawing around a side plate. Fold this in half.

2. Cut a strip of card (for the back) the diameter of the circle x 2 cm (0.75") approx.

3. Cut out your pointer from card to about 3 cm (1") longer than the radius of your circle and about 1 cm wide (0.4").

4. Cut out another circle of card approx. 9 cm (3.5") across.

5. Flatten the big card circle and measure the centre point (for your pin/fastener) just above the fold and mark with pencil.

6. Make a mark in pencil opposite the pin mark at the top outer edge and then eight more equidistant marks (see picture). When correct, go over with pen.

7. Write the words (or type, print and stick on) WORSE THAN, CENTRED, BETTER THAN and I MATTER! in the places shown.

8. Write the word EGOMETER at the edge of the smaller circle and stick this circle on the back of the larger one with the word showing at the top.

9. If temporarily using a drawing pin, carefully stick this through the bottom of your pointer into the central mark by the fold and put Blu-tack on the back.

10. When you have a paper fastener, make a hole through the end of the pointer and twizzle the paper fastener to make the hole round. Insert the paper fastener (with pointer) vertically through the place marked and open the split pins at the back.

11. Fold the circle again so that it stands.

12. Take the last long strip of card, bend both ends in by about 4 cm (1.5"). Glue these ends to the back to stabilise the Egometer. Make sure the front face is angled backwards slightly… Voila!

~ Design by IAN FENWICK AND CARMELLA B'HAHN

* The Practice *

Ego Watch

Take the time to make an Egometer. It *will* be worth it! Set the pointer to **Better Than** and brainstorm in your journal ways in which you bolster your sense of self by making yourself better than others. Do likewise with the pointer at **Worse Than.**

Now feel into and answer:
  ◆ What do I sense in my body when I put myself up and down?
E.g. you might sense your chest puffing out a little when feeling better than, or your shoulders slumping when feeling worse than.

If you have a lot of "worse than" thoughts, it's likely that you have a tendency to disappear and let your own needs be usurped by others. If so, you will benefit from cultivating a stronger sense of Self. This Self says, *I MATTER BECAUSE I EXIST* (not because of my achievements) and is able to communicate clearly without having to assert power over others or diminish its own importance.

During "Ego Watch" Week
1. Use your Egometer. Place it in the heart of the house; take it to work; have it prominent in your car if your driving is affected by your ego. You will know where it is needed. When you catch yourself doing a "better- or worse than" comparison, move the pointer from centred. Pay attention to your feelings when expressing off-balanced ego and note what triggers you. Consider catching yourself in action as a call back to centre... and smile.

2. Notice questionable ego behaviour in others. Politicians often blatantly belittle other parties to enhance their own specialness.
Be aware of feeling "better than" when catching others in the act!

3. Practise speaking from the clear sense of "I MATTER".

Review what you have learned. What do you intend to do differently?

Supportive Resources: *Inside-Out Healing*, Richard Moss.[9]
A New Earth, Eckhart Tolle.[10]

Who's Driving?

Holding the wheel of our life

---

* Opportunity *

To release thought-made, draining emotions
and move towards external disturbance
being like water off a duck's back.

---

*If it's never our fault,
we can't take responsibility for it.
If we can't take responsibility for it,
we'll always be its victim.*

~ RICHARD BACH
(Author)

TIP FROM HR STUDY GROUP

*The practices rely on you having thoroughly read and
understood the accompanying text.
Repetition works.*

Who or what is responsible for my emotional state? The answer massively impacts our relationships. The perception that the external world is responsible for our state of being, turfs us out of the driving seat of our life into the passenger seat, where bags of resentment are packed about our feet.

Passenger Seat Statements

- He *made* me feel…
- They should/not have…
- Their behaviour is…
- My childhood wasn't…
- No one understands me.
- It's unfair.
- People don't…
- My parents didn't…
- You never …
- Others… and therefore I feel upset.

Most of us have been reared to believe that life pushes us into the passenger seat and out of reach of our steering wheel. The more dramatic the story about what happened to us, the more others are likely to condone and sympathise with our lack of control, which bolsters our resentment. When we justify our feelings, attempting to convince self and others that we are true victims to something, this keeps us in a place where we are unable to access our wisdom.

> Stating the oft quoted and much forgotten obvious:
> IT IS NOT THE SITUATION ITSELF,
> BUT OUR REACTION TO IT
> THAT CAUSES LASTING IMPACT.

If 50 people were caught in a train crash in the same carriage, there would be 50 reactions. These could range from taking calming deep breaths and focussing on helping others (creating a memory that will affirm his/her inner strength) to screaming panic due to running a frightening story of what might happen next (causing future flashbacks to that fearful moment).

A transformational shift can happen every time we realise we've put someone/thing external in control of our feelings. Changing our passenger seat thoughts to driving seat ones (see practice) will radically clean up our communication as we, and others, feel the relief of us taking responsibility for our behaviour and direction.

Lighthouse Keeper

I am the keeper of the light
in my own house
of shadows.

Will I save myself from the rocky life
or will my keeper-self
be sleeping
in the danger of the night?

Will my inner tower of strength
hold steady
or will I crumble
into the sea of forgetting,
blaming my downfall
on the weather
of the world?

The light in my house is dimmed
by myself alone.
I am the keeper
I am the sleeper
and
safe passage
rests
in my hands.

~ CARMELLA B'HAHN

* The Practice *

Who's Driving?

To get into the driving seat of our emotions we need to:
- Realise that our thoughts/beliefs create emotions
- Recognise the first trigger thought
- Change that thought to a driving seat statement.

In your journal, write about a situation that has triggered a difficult emotional response in you recently. Note the effect of these emotions on your ability to focus and how much they drain your energy.
See what you come up with when filling in the dots below:
.....happened (or s/he said) and I felt (or feel)..... because I think.....
I could respond differently by ..... (new behaviour).

For example, *An insulation salesman phoned at 11.30pm.* I stayed awake all night and *I felt* irate because *I think* that this is a punishable crime!

Once you have found the emotion-causing thought, find a driving seat way of perceiving this experience, e.g. I kept myself awake by feeding "hamster wheel" thoughts about the unfairness of the crime. The call only lasted one minute! In future, I'll catch the hamster wheel starting, watch any thoughts with interest, and maybe switch to a relaxing focus. Today I'll see if I can block nuisance calls.

Examples of Driving Seat Statements
- My response to life and its "weather" is in my hands.
- This happened! I open to any learning from it.
- I release others from having to understand, love and respect me.

Note: Being in the driving seat is about being centred, not about swinging to the opposite pole of having control over others or life.

During "Who's Driving?" Week
Engage with arising passenger seat thoughts. How do you feel when others make passenger seat statements? Review the week's learning.

Supportive Resources: *Pulling Your Own Strings,* Dr Wayne W. Dyer.[11]
The Gaslight Effect, Dr Robin Stern.[12]

Speak for Yourself

Owning our particular vantage point

---

* Opportunity *

To live a life with fewer arguments by
avoiding defensive, aggrieved reactions;
and to be more fully heard.

I risk an ego battle
if I don't retract my pointed finger
and find an "I" statement,

~ CARMELLA B'HAHN

PLEASE NOTE
"I feel that…" will be followed by a thought – a belief or opinion,
not a feeling.

Using "I" statements – speaking from and taking responsibility for our *own* experience – dramatically increases the probability of being heard. You might think it's picky, pedantic and doesn't matter whether you follow the suggestions below, but I invite you to practise on the small things and discover for yourself the degree to which

"I" STATEMENTS PREVENT CONTRADICTION AND CONFLICT.

"You" statements are usually an interpretation of someone's behaviour and can feel like a pointed finger. They frequently attract a defensive reaction and some level of argument. Examples below in italics.

You are so stupid.

"I" statement alternative: I feel angry about what you have *done* because it has had an enormous impact on my day.

You don't care about my feelings; you are always making me wrong.

"I" statement alternative: I get upset when you criticise me because I like to do things well and I feel exposed when you point out my mistakes.

"We" statements are often presumptive as well as untrue. How do we know what others think and feel? Rephrase if your words don't allow others to experience the same thing differently, e.g.:

We will all miss you terribly. (Someone else could be thinking: That's so not true. I won't, I don't even like him.)

"I" statement alternative: I will miss you terribly.

The use of "one" or the general "you" can sound a step removed, e.g.:

One gets upset when one's dinner is lukewarm.

Who is "one"? Are you speaking about yourself, or anyone in general?

You feel lost without your dog!

If you mean "I", why not say "I"?

Personal Opinion masquerading as fact is a normal way of speaking, e.g.:

This curry is phenomenal! (Other's view: Ugh, this is horribly hot.)

"I" statement: I'm loving this curry, are you?

Communicating is such hard work. (Other: Learning is a delight.)

"I" statement: Communicating with you is challenging me right now.

What Doesn't Work

Joe: Brr… it's chilly! I'll close that window so we can be cosy.

Emma (having a hot flush): What! It's roasting in here.

What Does Work

Joe: I'm cold. Do you mind if I close the window?

Emma: Wow! I'm so hot. Can you leave it open a little and use this blanket?

* The Practice *

Speak for Yourself

"I" statements simply need to show clearly that we are speaking from our own vantage point. They can begin with another word.

You might like to test out:

- ◆ My feelings are...
- ◆ In my opinion...
- ◆ My take on this is... what's yours?
- ◆ My understanding is...
- ◆ From my perception ...

Use the previous examples, if necessary, to help you change the sentences below in your journal to "I" statements.

- ◆ You are so confrontational; you never agree with anything I say.
- ◆ You all know what's going on and don't want to include me.
- ◆ We are really stuck in our communication; we need to improve.
- ◆ That dress is horrible!
- ◆ That was a magnificent evening!

Think about what would happen if only "you" and "we" statements were used in a conversation or meeting.

During "Speak for Yourself" Week

1. Watch your language for use of "you", "we", "one" or any statements that could attract contradiction. Celebrate noticing, and experiment with using more "I" statements.

If you think it doesn't matter because people know what you mean, this may be true... or not. The question might be: How far do I want to train myself to speak cleanly and "own" my opinions? It is difficult to argue with "I" statements: only those who believe that people shouldn't think and feel for themselves will do so.

2. Observe your reaction when others, including media, use "you", "we" or "one" or personal opinions as fact. Answer in your journal:

- ◆ Do I choose to commit to using more "I" statements?
- ◆ If so, what is my strategy for remembering to use them?

What stands out from this week's experience that you could also use?

Love Without Falling

Loving from the inside out

---

* Opportunity *

To move closer to experiencing
unconditional love..

---

*Your task is not to seek for love,
but merely to seek and find
all the barriers within yourself
that you have built
against it.*

~ RUMI
(Mystic Poet)

PLEASE NOTE
*To reap the benefit of this section, you will need to give it
more time than some of the other sections.*

F alling in love can be intoxicating and enchanting; as can falling into any relationship that promises deep connection and mutual nurturing. However, if we are *falling* anywhere, the outcome could be painful. The normal quest for love seeks fulfilment from the outside in. The advanced love-challenge is to experience the opposite:

CAN WE LOVE FROM THE INSIDE OUT
WITHOUT LOSING OUR EQUILIBRIUM AND IDENTITY?

Janet Patti, an interviewee for my book *Mourning Has Broken,*[13] spoke of this when sharing the learning from her broken marriage:

> It is such a temptation to go unconscious and "fall" in love, wanting to believe the romantic fairy-tale image of meeting my other half, my perfect prince, who will complete me. Only disappointment will follow this way of being, because that dream is about what *he* will give, what *he* will be and do to fill my needs. Sooner or later he will fail to live up to my projections and will resent me trying to make him change to fit my image of what he should be. I am seeking to become inter-dependent now instead of co-dependent so that, whatever occurs in my outer life, I will have the inner resilience to avoid a repeat performance of the collapse of my world. I am focusing on who *I* am, what *I* have to give and what *I* need to create for myself to feel more whole. I have learned, above all, that no one else can fill my empty places.

This is a modern-day description of the inner marriage that spiritual teachers have called us towards through the ages. The call is to take responsibility for our own inner work and to realise our inherent wholeness, rather than believing that our better/other half is outside ourselves. Living as a half can give us a false sense of safety that will be shattered if he or she leaves or dies – and we all die.

We can't be and do everything ourselves; inter-dependence is a necessity, and every human being is surely fragile and unskilled in some way. But, at a fundamental core level, beyond persona and life history, we are complete, acceptable and loveable (see Identity Model – Week 3). Intimate relationships are perhaps best used for mutual support in finding this inner core and in discovering how to love and embrace the totality of who we are unconditionally.

THE LOVE PARADIGMS

Conditional Love (Fear is present)	*Unconditional Love*
I love you because you fulfil my needs.	I love you because you are you.
I compromise myself to fit what *you* want and need.	I stay true to myself as I take into account the needs and wants of us both.
I'll love you more if you change.	I accept you as you are.
I am right about your faults and I can judge you because I love you.	I aim to understand you and will lovingly support you to reach your highest potential.
I'm afraid to show you who I really am, so I'll keep part of myself hidden and protected.	I stand before you in my vulnerability and strength, my ugliness and beauty.
I love you because you are the right type/size/culture, etc.	I love you whatever "package" you come in.
What you don't know can't hurt you, so I'll keep quiet about my "transgressions".	Honesty and trust are the foundations of our intimacy.
If we love someone else, we can't love each other as well/as much.	Love is unlimited and we are free to express it appropriately.
Don't leave me!	We are free to follow our intuition about where we need to be.
This model scratches the surface of love and raises many questions for discussion.	

If you agree that unconditional love is what you are aiming for, ***without judging the outcome as good or bad***, use a scale of 0-10 on each line to appraise these aspects of your love in a relationship of your choosing. Then ask, "What would help raise my score?"

Model by Carmella B'Hahn

* The Practice *

Love Without Falling

Look at the two Love Paradigms and, as it says on the model, *without making a value judgement on your score* (this is about appraising where we are at, not about having to be an enlightened 10), take a primary relationship – romantic or otherwise – and systematically go through each of the nine lines of the model asking:

+ If totally conditional love is a 0 and unconditional love is a 10, where would I place myself on this scale in this relationship?
+ What would help me move towards unconditional love?

Write the results in your journal, particularly noting what aspects are working best and what is calling for attention. Highlight any action steps you think might enhance your way of loving this person.

Note: We can love someone unconditionally and know that living together would not or does not work practically. We might not even like their character or behaviour.

Now, turn the spotlight on yourself for a moment and consider this:

+ To what extent do I feel unconditional love when I focus on myself?

Take note of any connections between this self-love and the love you experience in the relationship you've been appraising.

During "Love Without Falling" Week
If it feels useful, share your findings from the Love Paradigms exercise with your loved one, or better still, do the exercise together.

Apply any actions you have decided to take to enhance your move towards unconditional love and test out using the following question in your life and relationship:

+ What would unconditional love do or say now?

Name one thing that stands out as important to remember from this week.

Supportive Resources: *Conscious Communication,* Miles Sherts.[14]
The Courage to Love, Malcolm Stern and Sujata Bristow.[15]

I'm All Ears

Understanding true listening

> ## * Opportunity *
>
> To create and experience deeper connections by
> listening, and to increase the likelihood that
> we will, in turn, be heard.

*Listening is miraculous
for both listener and speaker.
When someone receives us with open-hearted,
non-judging, intensely interested listening,
our spirits expand.*

~ SUE PATTON THOELE
(Family Therapist and Author)

At a speed-dating event, someone timed how long it took each potential mate to ask a question and start listening, then made the decision of who to date accordingly! If only we could absorb the wisdom of Greek philosopher, Epictetus, who said, *We have two ears and one mouth so that we can listen twice as much as we speak.*

BEING TRULY HEARD IS ALMOST A SURVIVAL NEED.

When someone really listens and shows that they have taken in what we have said, we feel cared about and connected with our listener. Listening is an art, a learned skill that requires much more than simply turning our head towards someone and hearing words with our ears. Many conversations are alternate monologues, with each person forming their next monologue as the other speaks.

As we have experienced from previous practices, when we listen *actively* with interest with our whole bodies, we can sense so much more than the words are saying. Remember to *feel* what is being spoken, to observe body language and to ask for more to enrich what has been said. Caroline Myss, wisdom teacher and author, says,

The conscious person reads energy first, matter second.
The unconscious person reads matter first, energy second.

Deep Listening Suggestions
- Complete the topic first raised rather than taking off on a connected track of your own. Until others feel heard they will find it difficult listening to you. "Tell me more" works well.
- Show curiosity and ask questions if you didn't understand.
- Keep your mouth closed more! Interjected verbal response can be distracting or influence what the speaker is trying to communicate.
- If it feels useful to show you have heard, capture the essence of what they have said and feed it back to them: "So are you saying…?"
- Notice their feelings and reflect, e.g. "You seem upset…"
- Avoid finishing their sentence or interrupting.
- Watch out for ego sabotaging your listening ability. You could be triggered by theirs or your own. No need to put them right. Listen!
- Acknowledge and appreciate the speaker in any way you can.

The Dynamics of Speaking and Listening

By Carmella and M'haletta B'Hahn

Speaker	The invisible line	Listener
Active Transmitter Strong signal projects to line		**Active Receiver** Fully focussed & listening up to line
Clear connection made		Content received
Stretched Transmitter Works hard to be heard		**Passive Receiver** Tired, uninterested, not now, habit…
Feels the strain	Misses content	
Passive Transmitter Tired, shy, ill, learned habit etc.		**Stretched Receiver** Works hard to hear
Full content unheard	Feels the strain	
Passive Transmitter Gives weak signal		**Passive Receiver** Not fully present & listening
Waste of time. Stop, change subject,	change mood or talk another time.	

* The Practice *

I'm all Ears

Explore the diagrams until you comprehend them. The speaker is on the left side, listener on the right and the line between is the central point between them. Note in your journal how your general listening skills relate to this model. In what position do you think you operate most – active, stretched or passive receiver? Make notes about how you change (if you do) in relation to specific individuals.

Copy the Deep Listening Suggestions in your journal. Star the ones you do well at already and mark those needing more attention.

During "I'm all Ears" Week
1. Look at and turn your body towards anyone speaking to you and practise actively listening right up to the midpoint between you. If you don't catch what is being said, ask for more volume or clarity.

2. Put into action as many as you can of the Deep Listening Suggestions that you marked as needing attention. Star those that you succeed in using and write about what worked or didn't.

Here's an example that combines the use of the first two listening suggestions – "Complete the Topic" and "Show Curiosity":

> **What Doesn't Work**
> I've had a hell of a day!
> *Really? So have I. My knee hurts and I've got a headache.*
> **What Does Work**
> I've had a hell of a day!
> *Why, what happened?*
> Well, when I'd got as far as town, I remembered I'd left the soup cooking and I had a doctor's appointment I couldn't miss...
> *Wow, that sounds difficult! What did you do then?*
> Yes, it was horrible, but I sorted it. How was your day?
> *Not good either. I fell over and really hurt my leg...*

Supportive Resource: *The Sacred Art of Listening* website.[16]

Wounds Listen

Noticing the filters through which we hear

*Only when I step out of my story,
into the now
can I listen
with pure hearing.*

~ CARMELLA B'HAHN

We can listen with "Wound Ears" filtering all that we hear through our difficult past experiences, our interpretations, beliefs and wishful thinking, leaving us swearing that we have heard things that were absolutely not meant. Or, we can listen through "Zone Ears", which stay in the present, hear beyond the words, are responsive to others' needs and are clear of all blockages.

Marshall Rosenberg's Four Ways of Listening – from the Nonviolent Communication teaching – uses the terms "Jackal" and "Giraffe" ears for "Wound" and "Zone" ears respectively, and explains this concept beautifully (my parentheses below). Read it through a couple of times and then look at the example to comprehend it fully.

Four Ways of Listening
1. Judging ourselves as right/wrong/good/bad
[When Wound Ears are turned inwards]

2. Judging others as right/wrong/good/bad
[When Wound Ears are turned outwards]

3. Sensing our own feelings and needs
[When Zone Ears are turned inwards]

4. Sensing for others' feelings and needs
[When Zone Ears are turned outwards]

WITH WHICH EARS AM I LISTENING?

When someone is criticising us or stating something we have strong feelings about, we have a choice: we can allow their words to stick to our wounds or our ego and consequently get caught in self-defence or attack – which meets no one's needs and heads us towards conflict – or we can listen for what that person might be feeling and needing behind their crunchy words.

If we are affected by our wounds to the extent that we cannot hear clearly, then it could be helpful to own up, e.g. "What you are saying is triggering something in me and I am not fully hearing you."

Example of Wound and Zone Ears

The Trigger

> *Dad had a lot of pain this afternoon and he tells me he wasn't given his medication.*

Zoe speaks to her sister who she left in charge
of their elderly father for the day.

According to the way she was listening, her sister could reply:

**Wound Ears
Inward**
(Blaming self)

> How stupid of me. You are right, I should have remembered he needed his medication at 3pm.

**Wound Ears
Outwards**
(Blaming other)

> I can't believe you didn't remind me. You know my memory is hopeless.

Zone Ears Inward
(Caring of self)

> I feel sad about making that mistake and I will find a strategy to help me remember his pills.

Zone Ears Outward
(Caring of other)

> Are you worried that I might do this again with more serious effects?

* The Practice *

Wounds Listen

Getting trigger-conscious is our first step towards clear, effective listening. Write in your journal examples of comments you find most difficult to hear – those that send you repeatedly into defence or attack. Whatever we struggle with, e.g. food intake, technology, illness, physical challenges, finance, power, will create instincts in us to overreact and therefore will probably mess up and complicate that particular subject in conversation.

A trigger that activates the Wound Ears of many teenagers is an adult asking – or *much* worse, telling – them to do anything. Requests for action often hit that unsure, powerless place of wanting and needing to be independent, but not quite knowing how. "Will you wash your dishes please before my guests come?" can be heard as, "So, I'm an incompetent imbecile who doesn't know I need to clean up."

Take one of the trigger comments that you have listed and follow the example pattern in your journal for each one. Write your most common Wound Ear reactions and think up potential Zone Ear responses to self and others.

During "Wounds Listen" Week
1. Get wise to anything that triggers your Wound Ears.
2. Practise activating Zone Ear responses (inward and outward).
3. If things go awry just say something like – Oops! I got triggered there… I'm going to start again.
4. Say to yourself, "Wound Ears!" when you notice others wearing theirs, and challenge yourself to listen more deeply for feelings and wants behind the words, e.g. people who sound rude usually believe their needs/wants are not being met.

Make notes of this week's most impactful insights. What will be helpful for you to use in future communication?

Supportive Resource: Nonviolent Communication (NVC).[17]

*A solid sense of self develops
from confronting yourself,
challenging yourself to do what's right
and earning your own self respect.
It develops* inside *you.*

~ DAVID SCHNARCH
(Author and Intimacy Therapist)

Recitation Practice

I have *emotions,*
but I am not *my emotions.*

I can feel and sense my emotions, and
what can be felt and sensed
is not the true Feeler.

Emotions pass through me
but they do not affect
my inward I.

I have *emotions* but I am not *emotions.*

~ KEN WILBER

WEEK 13

Joining the Dots

Understanding assumptions

> ## * Opportunity *
>
> To prevent ourselves from creating
> unnecessary confusion and
> misunderstandings.

*Until we can understand
the assumptions in which we are drenched
we cannot know ourselves.*

~ ADRIENNE RICH
(Feminist Poet)

How often do we catch ourselves and others playing "Join the Dots"? i.e., creating an untrue scenario from piecing together scanty bits of information. Making assumptions is a description of this.

To assume: To think that something is true, even though we have little or no evidence for it, e.g.

> You are speaking in a group about something important to you. One person is screwing up her face and another walks out. You assume they are reacting to what you're saying, and this second-guessing their actions makes you lose your thread. You might feel cross and then avoid these people because of the effect *they* had on you. Actually, one had forgotten his hearing aid and was frustrated not to be able to hear, and the other needed the toilet!

We need to become conscious of the assumptions we make if we want to save ourselves the grief that follows when we act as if the assumption is true when it's not. When we take our story of reality to others and rally their support for our imagined truth, things can get particularly sticky. Chinese whispers, which alter the truth, do untold damage including character assassination and false convictions.

Also, if many people join the available dots and reach the same conclusion, it doesn't make it true. We need to think for ourselves and avoid entering slipstreams created by combined agreement.

No doubt, most of us have at times also joined the dots to make fantasy pictures to fit our own desires, perhaps imagining someone we really like is feeling the way we want them to about us… or more.

We need to ask:
- Are my thoughts and stories based on fact?
- Did that person *actually* say or do what I imagined?

Sometimes assumptions are true, but perhaps it's best to assume that they are not, unless facts tell us otherwise.

IF IN DOUBT, FIND OUT.
ASK A QUESTION.

The Pweor of the Hmuan Mnid[18]

*Aoccdrnig to a rscheearch, it deosn't mttaer in waht oredr
the ltteers in a wrod are, the olny iprmoetnt tihng is taht
the frist and lsat ltteer be at the rghit pclae. The rset can be
a total mses and
you can sitll raed it wouthit a porbelm.
Tihs is bcuseae the huamn mnid deos not raed
ervey lteter by istlef, but the wrod as a wlohe.
Amzanig!*

The human mind naturally makes leaps to see the whole picture.
Sometimes accurate: sometimes not.

✻ The Practice ✻

Joining the Dots

You are a quarter of the way through the *Heart of Relating* course. Spend time revisiting in your journal your learning so far, reminding yourself of successes and things that you still want to apply in your relationships. (Your Join the Dots journal work will be done during the week itself as you catch yourself making assumptions.)

During "Join the Dots" Week
Be alert to the three things below. Make notes in your journal about your findings and review them at the end of the week.

1. Listen for assumptions you or others are making. Seemingly innocent statements and questions can cover unspoken assumptions, and the tone with which something is said can speak volumes, e.g.:
  My daughter hasn't called me for three days!
  (Assumption, daughter knows she "should" and is transgressing.)
  Are you in a romantic relationship?
  (Assumption that the other wants to be?)
  Is it raining there?
  (Assumption that the other doesn't want rain?)
  Do you have teenagers?
  (Assumption that they are hard to live with?)

2. Watch out for saying, "That means…" in your head to anything. It often precedes an assumption. Does *this* really mean *that*?

3. See if you can catch yourself reacting because you've made an assumption, e.g. you get defensive thinking a family member is angry with you because the door slammed.
CHECK FACTS and gather as many dots as possible to make the full picture, especially before you challenge someone, e.g.:
  When I heard the door slam, I thought you were angry with me but I wonder if that's really true?
  The response could be, "Haven't you heard the wind out there!"

What, specifically, will you continue to use from this week?

The Judge's Pendulum

Calming the right-wrong swing

* Opportunity *

To move towards freedom from the emotional
swings produced by judging, and to
consequently experience more harmony.

*When you try to push your rightness
toward another who disagrees,
no matter how right you are,
it causes more pushing against.
In other words, it isn't until you stop
pushing that any real allowing of
what you want can take place.*

~ ABRAHAM-HICKS
(Wisdom Teachers)

The kind of judgement that uses intelligent discernment to make the best choices possible is a vital tool for balanced human living. *Sitting in judgement* is completely different and can cause exhausting emotional swings in both the judge and the judged. The common habit of criticising each other creates a foundation of unsafety in relationships – often turning into tit-for-tat arguments. How can care be present and felt at the same time as unconstructive criticism?

It is the norm to judge, critically and morally, everything we encounter and this culturally embedded good/bad, right/wrong polarity swing works against the aspiration to love. Our good or bad categorisation creates a "now I'm happy…now I'm not" roller coaster. Imagine the emotional response to these statements: brilliant, we won the game!; damn it, we lost; you should have included me; great, there's no traffic jam; what a truly horrible day; I'm such a fool; she is much better than him; that was hopelessly incompetent.

The judge within is fed by the ego's need to know best and to be right. When we judge something as wrong or bad, we get to feel righteous in our rightness as we scout out the culprit to blame. And however mild our finger-pointing, it is likely to be sensed and will induce guilt, anger, or a defensive reaction unless the receiver is soundly in their core. When our sense of true self is strong, we can give our point of view, alongside other views that differ, without needing the ego boost of knowing best or winning the argument.

When we judge something as good or right, we praise, elevate and celebrate and it feels great. However, beware! When our "up" emotions are totally dependent on us getting the hoped for "positive" outcome, we are not yet retaining our balance from the inside, e.g. if our happiness depends on the sun shining, that phone call we are waiting for, or someone's praise, then we are being swung by the external. Acceptance is the key. For the pendulum to come to centre:

WE NEED TO ACCEPT THE EXISTENCE OF WHAT IS IN FRONT
OF US, NO MATTER WHAT, AND FIND ITS GIFT.
(See The Embrace –Week 43)

Story Time

Who's to Say if it's Right or Wrong?

There was once a wise farmer who owned a magnificent horse. One day, someone left the gate to the field open and the fine mare wandered off. He enlisted help from the villagers who commiserated by saying, "What bad luck to lose such a wonderful horse". The wise farmer replied, "Good luck, bad luck, who's to say if it's right or wrong that my horse is gone". A few days later, the mare returned accompanied by three wild stallions. The villagers talked excitedly of his good luck and the wise farmer responded, "Good, bad, who's to say what's right or wrong".

Soon afterwards, the farmer's son was out in the field breaking in the wild stallions when he was thrown from his horse and broke his leg. The villagers exclaimed, "Oh how terrible!" Yet again, the farmer said, "Good luck, bad luck, who can say what's right and wrong". A week later, war broke out and all able-bodied men from the village were called to service. The men all went to war except the farmer's son, who was no longer able-bodied. When the young soldiers from the village were all killed in an ambush, the villagers said to the farmer, "What good luck that your son's broken leg spared his life". And so on...

~ ADAPTED ZEN STORY

✳ The Practice ✳

The Judge's Pendulum

In your journal, make a note of a live situation where you think you are right and someone else is wrong. If there is nothing live, allow a memory from the past that still holds discomfort to surface. What thoughts arise about this person's transgression, e.g. He's so stubborn to ignore my advice; that was so stupid; she should have listened to me... respected my needs... remembered...!

Answer the following:
- ◆ What are the effects on my well-being when I think like this?
- ◆ Who is in charge of the thoughts that create the feelings?
- ◆ Will I choose to free up the blocked energy that this stance of rightness creates?
- ◆ Why does it matter? What am I trying to prove/protect?

Whoever you have "made wrong" is acting in the way they have learned to behave; no two humans are the same.

Brainstorm what you appreciate about this person to build a better feeling towards them. Imagine genuinely wanting to understand, and listening with interest and curiosity to their perspective. If they feel heard and appreciated rather than judged, they might well want to hear your perspective and any useful, caring feedback you can give.

Choose whether you will reach out to them, or let go and allow them to get on with their life in their way, and you with yours.

During "Judge's Pendulum" Week
Notice when you are tempted to make *anything* wrong. Practise acceptance and letting it go. If it matters, just give your information with "I" statements and listen deeply to the other's response.

Test out noting the cause and effect of something you don't like instead of judging it, e.g. What he's doing is not working to achieve what *I'd* like to see happen.

Capture any awareness about your own right/wrong pendulum swing.

Going into Space

Creating spacious connections

> ## * Opportunity *
>
> To allow a natural flow of sound, silence and
> space in order to experience
> interactions more fully.

Drawing on my fine command
of language,
I said nothing.

~ ROBERT CHARLES BENCHLEY
(Columnist and Actor)

What feels most natural -

sound,sound,sound,sound,sound,sound,
or
sound, silence, sound, silence, sound, silence?

⁓

Without space, can we truly integrate what's been spoken
and experienced so far?

⁓

Silence during communication
allows the emergence of wisdom and intuition.

⁓

If I don't say what's on my mind right now,
will it really matter tomorrow?

⁓

Speak if you can improve on the silence!

Fire

What makes a fire burn
is the space between the logs,
a breathing space.
Too much of a good thing,
too many logs
packed too tight
can douse the flames
almost as surely
as a pail of water would.

So building fires
requires attention
to the spaces in between,
as much as to the wood.

When we are able to build
open spaces
in the same way
we have learned
to pile on the logs,
then we can come to see how
it is fuel and the absence of fuel
together that make fire possible.

We only have to lay a log
lightly from time to time.
A fire grows
simply because the space is there
with openings
in which the flame
that knows just how it wants to burn
can find its way.

~ JUDY SORUM BROWN

From *The Sea Accepts All Rivers* – Miles River Press 2000

* The Practice *

Going Into Space

Breathe in for two seconds and then out for six seconds, and again… in for two and out for six. How does this feel?
Breathe in for six seconds and out for two… twice. How is this?
Now breathe in a natural way that feels comfortable.
Answer in your journal:

- What does this say to me generally about rhythm and space?

Read the Fire poem slowly, twice. Allow a response to the following questions to arise from your inner space:

- In what ways does this poem speak to me about my life and communication style?
- From what I have learned from the breathing and poem, what will I choose to test out this week in relation to spaciousness?

For instance, you could plan ten minutes silent integration time into the end of each day and ask, "Looking back on my day, what had heart and meaning for me that I want to remember?"

During "Going Into Space" Week
As well as applying the above, notice your breathing and speaking rhythm in action and, if appropriate, launch a personal enquiry about whether you are resistant to taking more (or perhaps less) space.

Social chat often moves fast, without much awareness and it is up to us to become conscious of any slipstream we find ourselves in. Check if you are content with the depth and speed of your interactions and notice how much space your conversations hold. Play with guiding communication you are unhappy with to a place and pace that allows the depth and flow you want… or maybe bow out of the conversation. You could request silence before responding if need be and take time out to mull over important decisions.

Capture any insights in your journal. What will you carry forward?

Supportive Resource: *Sabbath*, Wayne Muller.[19]

WEEK 16

My Media Message

What are we broadcasting?

* Opportunity *

To become aware of how the tone and content
of our expression feeds and affects our own
and others' well-being.

*Evening news is where
they begin with "Good evening"
and then proceed to tell you why it isn't.*

~ ANON

*How are
you
reporting
your emerging life story?*

What do you think of the news in the popular press and other media – our mouthpieces for local and world happenings? Perhaps you are appalled by the choice of depressing focus; impressed by the detail; bored by uninteresting content; entertained by the stories, scandals, celebrity mishaps; inspired by real life heroes and heroines?

Newspapers, websites, TV and radio shows, etc. are angled to reach a target audience and have a particular frequency or wave-length to which we are drawn... or not. Some news sources are truthful and responsible, but we have come to expect most to include distortion of facts, scenes of violence, loaded words, strong emotion, dubious research methods, melodrama, hype, conjecture and gossip with the occasional "cute new ducklings" story tacked on. This is our primary role-modelling for communicating news, which our children also absorb as normal, unless they are protected by guardians who present a stronger, more constructive message.

Every day, we broadcast a message about our personal world. Even if it is a silent movie some days, it still has a resonance, and whether or not anyone is watching or listening, the broadcast is still happening. Our body language, emotions, actions and words tell a story of how we are and what we value. The characters with whom we choose to interact are also crucial to the quality of our show, as is the scenery (the environment) in which we are acting out our lives.

WE ARE THE NEWSCASTER, EDITOR AND PRODUCER
OF OUR PERSONAL BROADCAST.
PERHAPS IT'S TIME FOR
A COMPASSIONATE CRITIQUE OF OUR TRANSMISSION.

If the cameras were on us 24 hours a day to make a reality show called, "This Is My Life", I wonder if we would behave differently and edit what comes out of our mouths? Would we be our natural selves once the cameras were rolling or would we use our best acting skills and put a "spin" on the truth? This week is about becoming conscious of the broadcasts we are both consuming and putting out so that we then have the choice whether to direct ourselves differently.

Story Time

Two Wolves

A Cherokee is telling his grandson about a fight that is going on inside himself between two wolves.

One wolf represents anger, envy, sorrow, regret, fearful thinking, greed, arrogance, self-pity, guilt, resentment, inferiority, lies, false pride, superiority and ego.
The other wolf represents joy, peace, love, hope, serenity, humility, kindness, benevolence, empathy, generosity, truth, compassion and faith.

The grandson thought about it for a minute and then asked his grandfather,
"Which wolf wins?"

The Cherokee simply replied,
"The one I feed."

~ A CHEROKEE TALE[20]

* The Practice *

My Media Message

Think of the news from the media that you "consumed" this past week. Make a list in your journal of any papers, shows and websites that you have connected with, and feel the impact that each had on you. Encapsulate these effects in a sentence or two in your journal, e.g.:

Newspaper found on train: felt emptiness, a voyeur, thoughts of having wasted my time.

TV news: Sent caring thoughts to those traumatised people, but couldn't get graphic images out of my head.

Film: Why, why, why did I watch it all? Disturbed and lost sleep even though I felt inspired at times.

Now answer in your journal:

♦ How does my media diet enhance or detract from my well-being?

Write about any changes you choose to make.

During "Media Message" Week

Imagine that cameras are following your every move this week. Each word you speak and every tone you use is being recorded. The gist of your week's drama will be published in your personal newspaper, on a TV documentary and also online for all to see – worldwide.

Watch out for which of the inner wolves (see Story Time) you are feeding most and see if you can imagine how your personal broadcast is being received by others.

Notice any behaviour that would embarrass you if made public and, at the end of the week, answer:

♦ What (if anything) will I choose to edit or change to make my broadcast more nourishing for myself and others?

Supportive Resources: *Taking Back Childhood*, Nancy Carlsson-Paige (Helping children thrive in a fast-paced, media-saturated world).[21]

Positive News – the world's first positive newspaper.[22]

WEEK 17

Juicy Gossip

Valuing discretion

> ### * Opportunity *
>
> To prevent the effects of indiscretion and to gain
> the trust of others by standing more
> in our integrity.

*If you wouldn't write it and sign it,
don't say it.*

~ EARL WILSON
(Writer/Columnist)

Gossip: Idle and indiscreet talk about others' personal business.

Gossip can be tantalizing, entertaining and difficult to resist. It can also fuel our feeling of specialness to have one up on someone else by knowing something they don't. Is anticipation and glee at the idea of telling a juicy titbit familiar? It takes two (or more) to gossip, and being an active, or even passive, listener condones the gossip's flow.

Gossip includes:
- Repeating something about someone that we imagine they would not wish to have disclosed without permission – including telling secrets to our spouse, best friend, or someone seemingly unconnected.

- Sharing something that makes someone else look bad, implies our superiority and reinforces our perspective of the truth.

- Starting rumour by conjecture – acting as if we know it's probably true, despite having only partial facts. Maybe we are correct but that is irrelevant to whether it's gossip.

- Rallying support for our own "rightness" (whether or not we are) by attempting to convince someone of another's faults.

Gossip is not:
- Passing on non-confidential news.

- Divulging and unburdening something bothering us to a supportive and non-judgemental listener, in confidence, with the intention to understand why it is affecting us.

WHEN WE ARE IN THE ZONE
GOSSIP FEELS UNCOMFORTABLE.

The effect of gossip can range from harmless to devastating. Without thinking, we can tarnish someone's character in the eyes of another and set off a snowball of untruth, often impossible to reverse. When we feel at home and at ease with ourselves, our conscience kicks in and gossip will struggle to slip out.

Would I be happy for this to be heard by or reported back to…?

Is this mine to tell?

"Gossip-Check" Questions

What is my motive for saying this?

What does my conscience tell me?

* The Practice *

Juicy Gossip

Gossip sells magazines, shows, etc. It is so ingrained in the western culture that we are often unaware when we are gossiping. Be compassionate with yourself as you become more aware this week.

Firstly, jot down in your journal any memorable incidents when you have been either at the receiving or spreading end of gossip.

Next, write about the outcomes of the gossip including any feelings you or others experienced.

During "Juicy Gossip" Week

See how often you can catch yourself saying something indiscreet, remembering to be gentle on yourself – few humans are gossip-free.

The "Gossip-Check" Questions are designed to help you hold your tongue if you are about to risk indiscretion. One of the risks is that what you say will be repeated back to the person concerned, out of context, with someone else's interpretation.

If you need to blurt out strong feelings about another's behaviour, choose your listener carefully, specifically ask for confidentiality and make it clear that you simply need to process your feelings.

Test out new responses when subjected to gossip

Hold others' "gossip transgressions" softly, without finger-pointing and say something like:

- I feel uncomfortable listening to this.
- If I was … I wouldn't want to hear someone saying that about me.
- Have you spoken to him/her directly about this?
- Are you sure this is absolutely true?

When we hold strong boundaries around participating in gossip, it can't get past us to spread further.

Use your journal to catch any awareness you have had about gossip.
How do you feel about diminishing gossip from now on?

WEEK 18
LARGER Than Life

Shrinking exaggerations

> ## * Opportunity *
>
> To experience others trusting our word more
> and eating less humble pie.

If you add to the truth,
you subtract from it.

~ THE TALMUD
(Sacred Jewish Text)

> ### TIP FROM HR STUDY GROUP
> *If you haven't done the week's practice, drop guilt, admit the*
> *truth and know that any discussion on the subject*
> *in hand can still be invaluable.*

There are charismatic characters who are magnetic, captivating, comfortable in their own skin and speak with truth and integrity but those I'm calling "larger than life characters" differ greatly. Yes, they can be very entertaining, but can use exaggerated speech and action simply to gain effect and attention, which often backfires.

To exaggerate: To represent something as larger or more important than is true – to overstate, e.g.:
- The whole room was weeping
- I fell on the floor laughing
- *Nobody* ever appreciates me
- *Everyone* loves everything I cook
- I am *never* going anywhere with my husband again
- I *always* have to clear up your horrible mess.

When we use sweepingly dramatic language and tell any size of lie, we can seed distrust that leads others to question what we say when it *is* powerful and true. Also, if we litter our speech with exaggeration, listeners can become weary of the effort of interpreting and responding to information that doesn't ring true to them.

Sometimes it won't hurt to elaborate a little, but there could be difficult consequences if our imprecise communication is taken literally, e.g. "There are *never* any taxis late at night from the airport" might cause a friend to book a different flight to ensure getting home, when actually what was meant was, "There are fewer taxis after 11pm and you might have to wait a while".

The art of exaggeration is absolutely fabulous for comedy, creative writing, jokes and drama, but perhaps the best way to bolster our self-worth is by feeling the sense of integrity gained from being real – expanded in Week 23 – The Real Deal.

WHEN WE ARE REAL, WE ARE NATURALLY POWERFUL.

Exaggerators can also be prone to catastrophising, i.e. putting a negative spin on something, making it appear worse than it is: "It's foggy and she's twenty minutes late. I'm phoning the hospital!"

*Exaggeration misleads the credulous
and offends the perceptive.*

~ ELIZA COOK
(Poet)

*Nothing makes
a fish **bigger**
than almost being caught.*

~ AUTHOR UNKNOWN

* The Practice *

LARGER than Life

Sit and ponder and make notes in your journal about whether you see yourself as someone who exaggerates or catastrophises. Did anything written so far on the topic resonate with you? Perhaps you tend towards the opposite and understate, thinking that this is modesty? Exaggerating and understating both tamper with the truth.

Suggestion: Avoid exaggerating about how much you exaggerate and programme yourself to laugh when you catch yourself out.

During "LARGER than Life" Week

1. Be alert to any ways in which you misrepresent reality by using exaggeration, catastrophisation or understatement. As you begin to notice any distortions of the truth, ask the simple question:

◆ Is this really true?

Correct yourself out loud in the moment if you dare, e.g.:

◆ You always keep me waiting… *sorry, the truth is, you are often late, not always.*
◆ I'll get back to you in the next 10 minutes… *actually, I'm unsure how long it will take, but I'll call as soon as I can.*
◆ Nobody cares about me…*well, I know that's not true, but right now I'm not in touch with your care for me.*

2. Listen out for yourself and others using words such as:
NOBODY   NEVER   ALWAYS   EVERYONE.

Take note of any other words you use or hear that overstate or understate reality in some way. Sense your bodily reaction when you say or hear any of these words.

3. Ask someone who knows you well whether you exaggerate, catastrophise or understate. If they say yes, ask how it affects them.

As always, make notes, review them at the end of the week and be clear about the most powerful insights as well as your intentions.

Time Travelling

Fully engaging with the present

* Opportunity *

To be able to engage fully with what is in front
of us now and to bring more presence of
mind to our communication.

*Having spent the better part of my life trying either to
relive the past or experience the future before
it arrives, I have come to believe that
in-between these two extremes is peace.*

~ AUTHOR UNKNOWN

PLEASE NOTE

*This section is not addressing the situation where you are
flooded by traumatic flashbacks, although the practice may
help to lead you back into the now.*

Time travelling is the stuff of sci-fi adventures. Or, looking closer to home, it's something most of us do most of the time, meaning that conversations are generally held without any of the participants being fully in the present. This, of course, also applies to much of our silent thoughts and self-talk which meander on an automatic roundabout of the past, or worry-wheel about how the future will turn out.

THOUGHTS ARE OUR MODE OF TRAVEL OUT OF THE PRESENT MOMENT.

It is one thing to inform the present by using the experience and lessons of the past constructively, but quite another to keep stoking past fires with the poker of our thoughts. Simply focussing in this way, we can create deep emotions and "negative" spirals that feel so real and yet we have set it all in motion by unconsciously inviting this into the present. Regret is thought-made; worry: thought-made; fear: thought-made; nostalgia: thought-made.

Was yesterday *really* better than this moment (which is being hijacked by the past)? Art Buchwald, an American satirist, said,

If you're hung up on nostalgia, pretend today is yesterday and just go out and have one hell of a time.

Unless we have a creative motive for feeding our conversations with what's past or in the future, why not stay alert to what is live in our senses *now* and speak about that? Doing so is the master key to living in the Zone from the inside out.

We all know that right now is yesterday's tomorrow and tomorrow's past. We know that when tomorrow comes, it will be experienced as our now. So when, if not now, will we stop travelling elsewhere? When will we stop tempting others into a lament of history, or seeking support for our worrisome imaginings of what's to come?

Happy-ever-after starts NOW with awareness and appreciation of what *is* here that *is* working. We can build constructively from a foundation of what is, whereas a base of what isn't will probably cause a landslide! Tomorrow will reveal itself in accordance with the focus we have on our present today.

Story Time

Missing People

For me to carry on telling stories, you need to know about my relationship with my most powerful teacher: death. My first son, Benjaya, drowned in a local river when he was five. People said in the way people do, "Time will heal". Well, lots of time has passed and I feel not only healed but deeply content with my life and expanded beyond recognition by the learning presented by loss on that scale. *However*, I am sure that it was not time that healed me.

Of course, many things contribute to healing, but recently I realised the major difference between me and some clients I see who are still in debilitating emotional pain decades after their children's death: They remain time travelling and I have ceased to do so.

I believe that there is a healthy grief; pure feeling that rises like a volcano and breaks us open to a very deep place. It needs to be expressed, bubbles up in the now and will pass through if allowed out. My observation is that the pain of natural grief is usually magnified by the bereaved when they travel into the past and future. For example, when someone dies, there is a tendency to go over and over the past, worrying about what could have been done better, getting stuck in time on the death itself, with "what ifs" and regrets causing untold emotion. And to add to that, there is facing the necessary death of all the stories about the potential future of the departed. Every thwarted wish, expectation and hope for a future that could have been but isn't, causes more grief.

My healing balm has been learning how to gently bring myself back to what's relevant now and focussing on my *present* relationship with my son. Whatever our beliefs about afterlife, we can choose to gather inspiring imprints left by our loved one's life and use this legacy to feed our present. Perhaps stepping into the now heals everything quicker than the march of time.

For the full story see *Benjaya's Gifts.*[23]

✳ *The Practice* ✳

Time Travelling

The antidote to time travelling, or "spacing out", is mindfulness – a Buddhist-derived practice (that includes meditation) which is booming in the West, presumably because it works to create more fulfilling lives. Jon Kabat-Zinn,[24] a much respected Mindfulness master, says,

> *Mindfulness means paying attention in a particular way; on purpose, in the present moment, and non-judgementally.*

Mindfulness Exercise
Please do this, even if it is familiar to you. Take a raisin or bit of tasty solid food. Close your eyes and feel it. Then examine it visually before eating it in *very* slow motion. Notice any thoughts and where they take you and keep coming back to your senses. Note that all your bodily senses rest in the present moment.

During "Time Travelling" Week
Notice your patterns of absence. Are you in the past or projecting to the future (including what you are going to say next), worrying, fearing, fantasising? Particularly check out whether you feel fully present with anyone about whom you are making good or bad judgements. Perhaps you are time travelling into a made up storyland about the situation or person.

When you find yourself on a mind journey, gently come back to your senses with a reminder, "I'm Time Travelling". *Be with* what's happening right now or you will miss it, like the full taste of food. Focussing on your breathing works well to bring yourself back.

Ask yourself at the end of the week:

- What is my most compelling travel destination and do I want to keep going there?

Be alert to the difference between time travelling on purpose (to make plans, prepare for future events, or to entertain yourself) and when you are unconsciously meandering out of the present.

What actions do you choose to make regarding Time Travelling?

WEEK 20

Who Said That?

Releasing tribal programming

* Opportunity *

To stand in our own truth, beholden only
to what feels right to us.

*Thinking
is like loving and dying.
Each of us must do it for ourselves.*

~ JOSIAH ROYCE
(Philosopher)

PLEASE NOTE

*This could be a very emotive topic that attracts guilt or blame
according to the degree of our personal imprinting. Remember
that all of us inherit programming from someone else who
inherited theirs. Compassion could be useful here.*

As children, we were like sponges. We automatically absorbed both the overt and covert messages of the behaviour that surrounded us. Who hasn't observed a little one perfectly mimicking adult behaviour in play or heard a child repeating with glee something like f***, f***, f***, when s/he realises the naughtiness of it? Big people – including the media – are seen as fountains of truth by little people, however confusing the messages. Children's advertising relies upon them believing what they see and hear.

Throughout our life, our programming – useful and otherwise – will perpetually spill out or inwards, often as advice or an admonition, without us realising that it is not our own voice speaking. Our sponges need squeezing out by catching the voices we have absorbed that masquerade as truth, and by asking questions such as:

> WHOSE VOICE IS THAT AND DO I BELIEVE IT?
> HOW CAN I STOP PASSING THE DAMAGE ON?

Was mother right that I will "catch my death of cold" by going out with wet hair? Dad said, "alcohol drowns sorrows", but does it work for me? Am I stupid because I express my intelligence differently from my brother? Will the world stop if I defy convention because I can't find matching socks and hate the feel of a tie round my neck? Who made up these rules and where is *my* choice in the matter?

Superstitions are excellent examples of absorbed messages; many of them are ancient, as if in our blood. It's not wrong to hold them, especially feel-good traditions like blessing someone when they sneeze, but the question again is, "Is this *my* truth?"

Does it really create bad luck to have an open umbrella or peacock feathers in the house (if so I'm cursed), walk under a ladder or spill salt? Is good luck manifest by touching wood, seeing a black cat, having a horseshoe over the door or finding a four-leaved clover?

Our challenge is to become conscious of the cultural voices within us and to make our choices without over-reacting *against* what we see as negative conditioning, which will swing us to the equally imbalanced opposite pole.

Story Time

The Ring of Whose Truth?

I was listening to a CD by medical intuitive Caroline Myss[25] in preparation for presenting a *Conscious Communications* workshop. She was speaking of a necessary step towards self-awareness: unplugging our circuits from the tribal databank.

She states that we are unconsciously programmed from birth by our "tribe" with powerful thought-forms such as: how old we should be when we marry; whether inter-racial unions are good or bad; the process of ageing; work ethics; cautions about saving money, avoiding risks and being too spontaneous.

Caroline was challenging me to discover what external forces and thought-forms still had authority over me. Are there voices of family or ancestors guiding me without my awareness? Do I, as she is suggesting humanity en-masse does, run my behaviour through a filter such as: "What would *they* say or think of me?", before I act?

I consider myself quite independent and free to follow my own inner voice when making decisions and I couldn't find a personal example to share with the workshop participants… until I was dressing on the morning of the course. I felt a familiar wave of disappointment that I can't wear more than one of my favourite rings at once because they don't fit my available fingers. Then a sudden realisation hit me – *all* of them fit the third finger of my left hand, which had been ring-less since I stepped out of marriage. I laughed out loud and jumped about the room with that finger in the air shouting, "Whose finger is this?" Who is telling me I can't put a ring on it? Do I care that my tribe has claimed this finger since the 9th century as a place to show my marital status? Do I dare to fly in the face of tradition and display any ring I like on that finger? I said, "I DO" as I placed my favourite ring on the third finger of my left hand and felt as if I had married an unclaimed part of myself.

Now I can choose *when* to put a ring on that finger and when to avoid giving a false cultural message.

* *The Practice* *

Who Said That?

Make a list of the most influential people in your early years: family, guardians, teachers, etc. These are the ones who possibly still live in your head. Note down any sayings or advice you associate with them that spring to mind. Perhaps they held strong ethics or opinions about work, marriage, sex, the body, ageing, money, etc. Circle anything you feel you have absorbed from them and the time/culture they lived in. Discussing this with someone first could help.

Choose what you want to keep and what you want to release to help you inhabit yourself fully. Maybe put a big **R** next to those you want to release and a **K** for keep. The influences you keep could be seen as part of that person's (or your culture's) legacy – wisdom you will continue to share because it rings true.

During "Who Said That?" Week
1. Stay alert to the "tribal" voices of influence that you have written about – as well as others you haven't remembered – arising in your communication or behaviour. Just noticing, *That's my mother's/grandpa's/culture's voice,* without judging it, will bring it to consciousness and loosen its power. You can then question whether you believe it and want to own it. Some things you will already have made a Release or Keep decision about.

Each time you notice an unhelpful influential voice, look for a way you will recognise it next time it raises its head. Notice your body sensations and feelings when under the influence, e.g. you might have a sense of feeling snide and could say in future, "Father Snide's here again". Naming the intruder can be amusing and helpful. Then see if you can breathe the culprit away. Feel your feet on the ground and/or use any of your own ways of re-finding your core self.

2. Sense when others may not be speaking their own truth. Perhaps check, e.g. "Could that be your mother speaking?"

What actions will you continue from this section?

WEEK 21
Thought-Bodies

Clearing our mental fields

---

* Opportunity *

To come clear, clean and open to each interaction,
thereby giving it the best possible chance
of being nourishing.

You have a mental image, not only of who the other person is, but also of who
you are in relation to the person
you are interacting with. So you are not relating to that
person at all, but who you think you are is relating to
who you think the other person is and vice versa.
The conceptual image your mind has made of yourself
is relating to its own creation, which is the conceptual
image it has made of the other person.
The other person's mind has probably done the same,
so every egoic interaction between two people is in reality
the interaction between four mind-made identities
that are ultimately fictions.
There is no true relationship.

~ ECKHART TOLLE
(Author and Consciousness Teacher)

Thought vibrates at a frequency that we can sense to a degree, but cannot see. But if we *could* see thought-bodies (the mental substance from which words are shaped) what would they look like? Maybe constantly changing, with intricate patterns, swirls, thicknesses, weights, colours and degrees of translucence. We are deliciously complex, and every person with whom we relate brings out different patterns of thought and aspects of who we are.

Language is littered with labels that we use to describe each other's thought-bodies and their accompanying emotions: warm, cold, heavy, wet, thick, slippery, sharp, slow, wishy-washy, vibrant, clear, solid, all-over-the-place, blue, etc. Sometimes we stick these labels on people and situations as if they describe the whole, even though we rarely see more than one facet of anything at a time. We would need multiple, X-ray eyes to see every facet of the whole at once.

Influences – such as our current circumstances, health, amount of sleep, the topic of focus, our history, time limits, and distractions – affect every interaction. And so, when we hold someone in our mind the way we experienced them before, and subsequently communicate through that mental picture, we are no doubt, as Eckhart Tolle suggests in the quote, preventing the unfolding of a true relationship.

Our thoughts about someone can easily be coloured by another's opinion before we have exchanged a word with them, e.g. "Just to warn you, he's a bit tight and uncommunicative but his wife is kind and bubbly". Whether favourable or not, others' opinions will tint the way we relate from the first moment, if we allow it.

THE CHALLENGE IS TO OPEN AFRESH WITH EACH PERSON
WE MEET BY DROPPING OUR PRECONCEPTIONS.

We might have some investment in holding someone in our mind in a particular way because it allows us to continue a behaviour that we don't want to stop. We might not want to show ourselves transparently either. What matters is that we know that it's our choice, and that each choice will affect the nature of the relationship.

Story Time

Thought-Bodies

People she knew now lived wrapped up in thought-bodies, which was why they could not understand silence. The thought-bodies got in the way. They were like thick black clouds through which the purity of silence could not enter, and they kept people captive and dulled. Sometimes there were gaps in the thought forms. Amma, for instance, had many gaps, and these gaps were the silences of perfect love. Thatha had hardly a thought-body at all and babies had none. Little children had thin ones and David's, because he loved her, was transparent. Savriti felt these thought-bodies so clearly they were almost tangible, like thick walls of brambles and they hurt, almost, because you wanted so much to get behind them and they pricked...

Savriti had grown up amongst the English... They lived entirely in their thought-bodies, which were actually outside of themselves. They believed these thought-bodies to be much more real than what was inside. It was as if a butterfly wrapped up in a cocoon thought the cocoon to be itself! It was a form of blindness; it was a form of death.

Savriti had a thought-body too, but hers was like gossamer, like the shawl she sometimes threw over her shoulders or over her head, or waved in the sun when she danced, or simply threw over a bush to be free. It did not bind her down; sometimes it made her sad or bashful... but mostly her thought-body was composed of happy, translucent thought-lace, and delighted in the play of living things and their beauty.

Extract from *Of Marriageable Age*, by SHARON MAAS.[26]

✳ The Practice ✳

Thought-Bodies

Allow a clear memory to arise of a recent, highly enjoyable verbal interaction. Temporarily suspend any doubt and play with the idea of thought-bodies. Imagine how yours and the other person's thoughts might have looked during this interaction. Using colours, express the patterns in your journal, and write down anything that comes to you.

Now allow a memory of a difficult, intense interaction to arise, and play some more with colours and shapes. What do you imagine the thought-bodies of all concerned, including yourself, looked like during this interaction? Did anyone do or say something specific that you think might have changed your thought-body?

During "Thought-Bodies" Week
1. KEEP CLEARING your mind of preconceived thoughts about anyone and anything. When labels and judgements leap in, usher them out and imagine the immense potential that can arise from holding an open, expectant space in which you imagine others in the best light you can. Note what happens in others when you do this. Here's an example:

> There is a telephone service provider with whom I and others in my community have had immense trouble, leaving us without phones for weeks and the Internet continually going down: no one taking responsibility; confusion all over the place. Just saying the company's name seemed to manifest heavy, black clouds of powerlessness, through which we were then communicating in sharp and disdainful tones. Eventually, I decided that I couldn't change the company's ways of operating but I could dissolve my heavy thought-forms and treat the next engineer who showed his face with kindness, opening to the idea of him easily sorting everything. He came, was funny, fixed everything, gave me a free device and sorted a cheaper contract!

2. Reread the Story Time piece and imagine the general state of your thought-body.

Be specific about any changes you choose to make.

For decades I followed
self-improvement and spiritual paths,
agreeing that I needed
to perfect myself.
The joke, I've discovered, is that
the key to feeling whole
lies in welcoming my "imperfections".
Acceptance has brought
both change and peace.

~ CARMELLA B'HAHN

Recitation Practice

I have *thoughts,*
but *I am* not *my thoughts.*

I can know and intuit my thoughts,
and what can be known
is not the true Knower.

Thoughts come to me
and thoughts leave me,
but they do not affect
my inward I.

I have *thoughts*
but *I am* not *my thoughts.*

~ KEN WILBER

WEEK 22

Please, Please Me

Changing unreal niceness

> ### * Opportunity *
>
> To become more energised by learning to
> give in a way that nourishes us.

I say yes when I mean no
and the wrinkles grow.

~ NAOMI SHIHAB NYE
(Poet and Novelist)

> ### TIP FROM HR STUDY GROUP
>
> *Are you tuning out when you think you know something*
> *already? Pre-judging the result? Just release that thought,*
> *do the practice and be open to new awareness.*

When we trade niceness with others, clear communication stops. The pleasing pattern is summed up by the Beatles in their song *Please, Please Me* (Come on, come on, come on, come on, please, please me woah yeah, like I please you). Saying "yes" when we want to say "no" is especially tempting with people we want to impress as well as in intimate interactions when our desires do not fit with our partner's. The "let's be nice" collusion soon breeds suppressed resentment as we begin to feel the impact of subjugating our needs.

Of course, it is natural to want to please others and to feel good when they appreciate us, and, if others behave in a way that pleases us, we will naturally appreciate them. This interchange helps us feel warm towards each other. But beware of the co-dependency trap! If our motive to please another is the *need* for appreciation, when he or she doesn't like something about our behaviour, we may feel a loss of self-worth, angry, let down, and perhaps an urge to make things "right" again. Also, in this mutual trap, if the other behaves in a way that we don't approve of, we will suffer to some degree.

Back we go to Who's Driving? – Week 8. Are we being driven by what we think others want of us in a classic "outside in" behaviour? Are we tempting others into the co-dependent trap by wanting or expecting them to please us? The communication of those who are displaying the pleaser pattern is as clear as mud!

The desire to please and avoid boat-rocking can also lead us to become silent witnesses: we experience a situation that does not sit right and yet we do not speak up to help stop it. What will give us the courage to speak our truth? All roads lead to "the Zone".

WHEN WE FIND OUR CORE
WE WILL ACT FROM WISDOM AND INTUITION
RATHER THAN FROM FEAR OF DISAPPROVAL.

The games will cease and the mud will clear when we practise standing in the Zone, beyond the frightened ego, and when we dare to be truly authentic (see how in next week's The Real Deal).

Story Time

Giving or Giving In?
Kelly Bryson[27]

You can see from someone's body language, if you watch carefully, whether they are *giving in* to you or *giving* to you. I believe only about 20% of communication is verbal and 80% is non-verbal and energetic. There's a huge difference between mental verbal consensus and energetic, body energy consensus. In our community we have a rule that no one is allowed to give in – go along with it if they are not on board with a full YES. This is the beginning of resentment. If you stay in dialogue a couple more minutes you can find something win/win that has energy for both of you.

Here's an example: I came home the other day and my daughter said, "Daddy, let's play a [racquet] game". I said something violent, I said, "OK" without any enthusiasm. She said, "No way Daddy, you are giving in. When you say it like that, you will play the game like this, na, na, na, na, na." She was waving her hands about with low energy. "It's boring and no fun when you are not into it. Keep negotiating." I decided to practise transparency and tell her the truth: "I'm tired. I just got home from playing basketball and I'd love to hang out with you, but I don't want to do anything heavy-duty physical." She said, "Daddy, that's fine, all you have to do is lay in your bed, I'll make things and you can tell me how beautiful they are." That worked wonderfully for us, we were both on board. Our energy was high and what I call "the frequency" of our connection went way up once we found something we were both 100% behind.

We need to stay with the process until the frequency gets strong. I call it FRED: Frequency Resonation Energy Dynamic. In the community we ask each other, "How's Fred and what does he need?" Sometimes we'll get stuck trying to resolve a problem because the FRED is low, so we'll quit trying and come back to it once we've changed the frequency by doing wild dancing or something.

* The Practice *

Please, Please Me

Did you take in the power of Kelly Bryson's story? If not, I invite you to read it again. By attempting to please others, being good and agreeing when we are not feeling a full, resonant YES, we create a na, na, na experience. Our non-verbal messages will communicate our resistance, even if our mouth says yes.

Contemplate and/or brainstorm in your journal any times when you have said yes when you felt a no.

- Who are the people you are more likely to do this with?

- Is there any situation where you have said yes at your own expense that you could rectify now that you are more aware of it?

E.g. When you asked me what I was doing on Saturday and I said, "nothing", I felt that I couldn't then refuse when you asked me to go out, so I said yes, when I wanted to say no. The truth is that I was excited to have a relaxing night off. Would it work for you to go out on Sunday instead?

During "Please, Please Me" Week
1. Reread the wrinkles quote and ask the image of wrinkles (or a strong image of your own choosing) to show itself as a signal every time your inner scanner notices a wavering yes in yourself or others.

When you sense a wavering yes
- Ask, Am I/they "giving in" or "giving to"?
- Keep talking until an elegant solution has had enough space to arise and you feel a clear resonance with the decision.
- Ask for or suggest they take more time and come back to it.

2. Ask someone you are close to if they will commit with you to being alert to any "giving in" patterns between you and to finding a full YES before making agreements. This will support you to bring any "Please Me" patterns into the open.

Supportive Resources: *Don't be Nice, Be Real,* Kelly Bryson.[28]

The Real Deal

Discovering the power of authenticity

---

* Opportunity *

To experience relationships that are free
of game playing.

---

*Your only obligation in any lifetime
is to be true to yourself.*

~ RICHARD BACH
(Author)

When describing someone as "the real deal" we could also say that they are authentic, honest, trustworthy, believable, genuine, congruent and reliable. The "sound" of someone being real is particularly satisfying because the words, tone, and non-verbals all match and ring true. Consequently, the listener might well find the speaker riveting, disarming, surprising and safe to be around.

Much of our conditioning negates authenticity:
- Being nice to each other
- Stiff upper lip
- Avoiding disapproval
- Making a good impression
- *Needing* to wear make-up
- Avoiding conflict
- Seeing vulnerability as weakness
- "Saving" people's feelings
- Certain cultural manners
- *Having* to be fashionable

Also, sprinkling too many clichés, off-the-shelf comments or common platitudes in our speech won't help us become the real deal and can be irritating. For example, "There's plenty more fish in the sea", "You can't teach an old dog new tricks", "It will all be all right, you'll see". To be authentic we need to stay in our *own* feelings and responses as we experience each unique moment. When difficulties arise, we can build our coping muscles and help things to move on by squarely facing and naming what is happening now. This opening to reality also allows our intuition and hidden strengths to emerge.

PUTTING THE LID ON ANYTHING CREATES PRESSURE.

What is authentic communication?
- It speaks of our *own* experience using "I" Statements
- It courageously tells our truth (at an appropriate time)
- It includes our bodily senses and feelings as well as thoughts
- It expresses what is happening in and around us *now*
- It is clear and direct
- It is supportive of others, even when challenging them.

We do not have to be in the Zone to be real, although it helps. We *do* need to be *aware* when we are out of balance, in order to be authentic about the state of being we are in – see the practice page.

Story Time

Popping False Bubbles

After my son died I had some bizarre encounters where avoidance of reality in the communication was so blatant that it was painful. The unspeakable hung awkwardly in the air, resulting in feelings that were the opposite of what was desired. For example, a few weeks after Benjaya's death, I met a friend in my village, who I will call Zoe. I had seen her cross the road once when she had seen me coming, otherwise I hadn't seen or heard from her since his death. Here's a shortened version of our first communication:

Zoe: (Said with eyes darting all over the place.) Hello, it's good to see you I'm just getting Dad's shopping. It's freezing out isn't it? I think I might be getting a cold and I've only just recovered from the last one.

Me: (Steering her by the arm towards the shop.) *Come on, let's get into the warm then. And by the way, just in case you're wondering, it's really fine to mention Benjaya.*

Zoe: (Turning to engage fully and reaching for my hand.) I'm so sorry, I was rambling because I'm nervous and don't want to upset you. I guess it feels safer talking about the weather. Would you like me to pop over for a chat some time? I really do want to find out how you are.

The false bubble had been popped by a few simple, real words and we were connected again. She did come to visit me and told me how nauseous she'd been feeling when imagining what life must be like for me. She admitted to having avoided me because she had no idea what to say or how to handle her own emotions. This honest communication, which allowed her vulnerability to be seen and accepted, created a compassionate flow between us.

We do not need to know the best strategy or way to behave, just telling it as it is in the moment leads us to the next steps. Touch can also be used effectively, with or without words.

* The Practice *

The Real Deal

It is time to take an honest look at our primary relationships. Write in your journal the names of all those with whom you relate regularly – family, workmates, friends. Create your own system to show visually how authentic you rate each friendship on the authenticity scale, and star any relationships that you want to become more real.

During "Real Deal" Week
1. Refer to "What is authentic communication?" and test out being as real as you can – especially with those you have starred.

Example of an authentic response when off balance
I'm feeling upset and need to express what's disturbing me before I focus on anything else. I'll say it in the best way I can, given my feelings. When you told me at the last minute that you couldn't make it, I felt shocked because I believe you hadn't considered the impact on me, which was severe. Can I tell you about it?

Example of what to say when lost for words
I have no clue where to go with this conversation right now and I feel exhausted by trying so hard. Can we stop a minute, do something different and come back to this later?

To reiterate: You don't have to work it out in advance; just be real.

2. Making the Authenticity Pact
If you can, find someone who is willing to make an on-going authenticity pact with you. You would both agree to act as honest mirrors for each other, sharing anything that you think is in the other's best interest to know – especially your blind spots that you can't see without a mirror. Agree to share sensitive feedback at a time when you can both be fully present with each other and are not emotionally charged. (This pact has saved many a relationship!)

3. Ponder this quote by novelist, Barbara Kingsolver:
The truth needs so little rehearsal.

Clear as a Bell

Speaking with crystal clarity

---

* Opportunity *

To increase the likelihood of
being understood and fulfilling
ours and others' wants and needs.

All my life, I always wanted to be somebody.
Now I see that
I should have been more specific!

~ JANE WAGNER
(Comedy Writer)

PLEASE NOTE
We differ in how we find clarity. Some feel their way, some
think their way, and some combine the two —
all at different speeds. Make allowances for this.

When we are clear as a bell, we have the best chance of being heard. Who? What? When? How? Where? Why? If what we say leaves others frowning quizzically or asking questions to clarify, we need to be more specific. Lack of information is the breeding ground of misunderstandings. If a father says to his young son, "Want to come and get some fish with me, Freddy?" and his son has been promised a fishing trip as soon as he is big enough to go, imagine the scene when Dad pulls up outside the supermarket instead of the river.

We need to be particularly specific with any directions we give. On a singing camp I heard the head cook say to her voluntary team, "Soak the rice first". Well, the 100 campers ended up with rice pudding instead of curry because she omitted three words, "in cold water"!

It works both ways. A common assumption many of us make is that we *should* understand from the amount of information given. Have you ever been physically lost, unclear about the directions you've been given, but didn't ask for clarification? We will continue being lost until we ask for, and get, specifics. We need to check with ourselves that we have fully understood any needed information before we move on.

Stating our needs, as well as recognising others' needs, can be extremely helpful as part of our clarity. Earlier, my son interrupted my writing flow to say, "Have you got any earplugs?" If he had said that he was trying to read a book on his laptop over the distracting buzz of a fan, I would have jumped up to help rather than saying, "I'm writing, I'll get them later".

BE SPECIFIC: YOU GET WHAT YOU ASK FOR.

If we do not know all the details of what we want, we can focus on what we *do* know – and particularly on the specifics of the way we want to feel. For instance, when wanting to find a new home without a clue what it will look like, we could say: "It will be quiet, with open spaces and trees all around, I will feel peaceful and I'll know it's mine because I will feel a YES! in my body when I walk in the door."

Be Specific!

* The Practice *

Clear as a Bell

If you have a bell in the house, put it somewhere prominent so that you can see it this week. If not, draw, the outline of a bell with the words BE SPECIFIC on it and put this on your fridge or other visible place as a reminder.

During "Clear as a Bell" Week

1. When you become aware of the slightest feeling of confusion or incomprehension, avoid joining the dots. Get specific so that you can respond appropriately to both the facts *and* the emotive content of anything that is being said.

Use clarifying questions

- ◆ Who? What? Where? When? How? Why?
- ◆ How are you feeling about that?
- ◆ It sounds like you mean… is this what you're saying?
- ◆ What do you/I really need here?

2. Become alert to the non-verbals of others in relation to them understanding *all* that you are saying. We tend to focus on and hear clearly what we want to hear and magically blank out the rest.

Clarify your own communication

- ◆ Have I given enough context and specifics to make myself understood without effort and second-guessing by my listener(s)?

Take the example of needing a baby-sitter: Opening with, "Are you going out tonight?" fails to include anyone's needs in the question. What if s/he is not going out but doesn't want to baby-sit? What if you might lose your job if you don't get cover for that shift?

Important: "I don't know" can be an honest and clear answer and allows the questioner to find clarity elsewhere.

Congratulate yourself for any extra clarity you created. What, specifically, worked well for you that you will continue to practise?

WEEK 25

Heart and Head Weave

Marrying feelings and reason

* Opportunity *

To connect more fully with others by becoming fluent in the expression of both feelings and facts.

*The heart
has its reasons
of which reason knows nothing.*

~ BLAISE PASCAL
(Mathematician and Physicist)

Becoming fluent in the language of both the heart and head will transform certain dysfunctional dynamics. The heart, through time, has been associated with women, but anyone with more feminine tendencies will use feelings as a primary source of understanding and relating to life. The head, generally speaking, is the natural realm of the male, but anyone with more masculine tendencies will use more reason and facts to make sense of life. This theme will be expanded in Bows and Arrows – Week 30, but for now, let's assume that whether male or female, we are aiming for heart and head fluency.

The heart realm includes: feelings; empathy/connection; the bigger picture; visual, auditory and sensory awareness; stories; metaphors.

The head realm includes: thoughts; facts; analysis; reason; logic; sequence; structure; practicalities; solutions.

Weaving head-based words between heart-based expression will usually have more impact than using only the heart or head, although sometimes a compassionate hug or simple fact alone will suffice.

The heart and head weave looks like this: Show you care and connect to the feelings behind any words. Gather facts, make sense of the situation and find solutions. Show connection and care again.

Take the example of going into a cafe for lunch. There's a choice on both sides of staying completely transactional or adding a little care that could create a feel-good interaction.

Transactional (head): "Table 6 is free." "*Thank you. I'd like a juice and sandwich please.*"… "Here's your bill, pay at the desk."

Heart added: "Table 6 is ready for your weary legs." "*Thanks, I am ready to drop. I'll have a sandwich and juice please. I expect your legs are tired too!*" "Too right!" … "*Thanks, that looks good. I hope you get a break soon.*"

OUR HEARTS LITERALLY TOUCH PEOPLE.

Neuroscientists have discovered that the heart has an electromagnetic energy field that stretches at least ten feet beyond the body and is 5,000 times bigger than that of the brain.[29]

Story Time

Weaving a Decision

When my second son, Asher, was thirteen, his father became clear that he wanted him to go and live in China with him and his new wife who had taken the job of her dreams in Shanghai. He made a strong case for what he wanted, based on a considered list of plausible reasons why it would be better than Asher staying with me in England. He called me with this list in hand and, I imagine, expected me to debate the pros and cons with him.

I felt instantly frightened by his list and approach, despite having an equally long one in my head in favour of the opposite view. Logical debate is not my strong point, and I have always had trouble understanding the purpose of playing a ping-pong match with balls of opinion when underlying feelings and intuition are left under the table. Playing that game I would surely lose.

However, I soon found myself fully engaged and on the edge of my seat when he answered my question: What do you *feel* about this situation; what does your heart have to say? He began to verbally recognise the pain that this separation would cause me, especially given the death of our first son. He divulged feeling torn apart between the needs of his wife and his son. He would have to lose one of them from his daily life if I declined his request. He reminded me that he had made a heartfelt commitment to Asher, before he was born, to give him everything that he had failed to give as a father to his brother, Benjaya.

I wept at this and my list paled in significance on the spot. I took several days to let myself fully absorb both the facts and feelings involved in this decision until I finally felt the "yes" settling in both my head and heart. It was clear to me that Asher's international education in Shanghai was made possible by his father's heartfelt expression joining with his reasoning. And yes, the separation was hideously painful, but I never doubted the decision for a second, given the foundations from which it was made.

(See further aspects of this story in Space Invaders –Week 32.)

⁎ The Practice ⁎

Heart and Head Wave

Do you think you are heart or head dominant, or equally fluent?

Here's an example for further clarification of what each sounds like: You've fallen down some steps and are badly bruised. A friend is visiting you soon afterwards and you tell him/her, "The pain is getting worse and I feel awful."

> **HEAD response:** How would you rate your pain on a scale of one to ten? I presume you are using arnica cream for the bruises and have called the doctor?
>
> **HEART response:** *Oh, that sounds hideous. I feel for you.*
>
> **HEART AND HEAD WEAVE:** *That sounds hideous, I feel for you.* I have some arnica cream if you want to try it. *I will do anything I can for you while I'm here because I want you to feel better.*

Write down how you feel on hearing each of these responses.

During "Heart and Head Weave" Week

1. Notice your heart/head tendencies and use any opportunity to practise weaving them by loosely following the pattern above.

2. With a partner, role-play your responses (as above) to their panic-filled statement below. Ask them how they felt after each response.

> **Partner says:** I've lost my car keys and I have to be at the doctor's in 15 minutes.

Repeat this process with you saying the following and feeding back to your partner how you feel about his/her three responses:

> **You say:** I have an important interview tomorrow and I'm really anxious because I can't find an outfit that feels right.

Share with your partner (and then write about) your heart/head patterns of speech, including anything you want to change. Note that a head response does not necessarily mean lack of care. It could be that care is just not expressed and so is not easily felt by the recipient.

Supportive Resources: Web article by Jay C., *Brain – Left or Right?*[30]

Take the Spinning Lady test to see if you are right or left brain dominant.[31]

Moons in Moccasins

Practising empathy

> ### * Opportunity *
>
> To expand our ability to care
> about those whose
> standpoint is different from our own.

*There's no one you
couldn't love
if you heard their story*

~ ANON

*D*on't judge anyone until you have walked two moons in their moccasins is a Native American proverb.

A Muslim version says, *To understand someone, you've got to walk a mile in their shoes, whether they fit or not.*

It can be easy to forget the obvious truth that each person is unique. Everyone has a different life experience, a different worldview and a different style of relating. However, there seems to be a common assumption that others think and operate like ourselves... and if they don't, they should. (Perhaps "should" should be abolished!)

The ability to experience life from our own standpoint, to be conscious of our own take on reality and to stay in our integrity without being swayed by others, is a vital part of relating well. It is a skill that we need to learn as youngsters – a constructive, inside out expression of our personal self. However, we can get stuck in a stance where what *we* want and believe is so strong that we are blinded to the standpoint others and our impact on *them*.

The success of our relationship with anyone – whether intimately involved, simply transacting, teaching, parenting, nursing, selling something or negotiating an agreement – is dependent on us having the ability to project ourselves into the other's shoes. Consciously taking another's standpoint and imagining experiencing the situation from their viewpoint is a technique used in many therapies. It creates empathy: the ability to identify and understand another person's feelings or difficulties.

When we are in the Zone (Week 4) with our Egometer's pointer at "centred" (Week 7), we do not compare or need to be right, and we naturally accept, even celebrate, another's difference. Diverse ways of being show us what we do or don't want in our own life and offer information that can help fine-tune our own values and behaviour.

CURIOSITY IS ONE OF THE BEST TOOLS
TO BUILD EMPATHY
AND TO DISCOVER THE VALUE OF OUR DIFFERENCE.

Story Time

Set Free by the "Enemy"

Rosalie Gerut[32] was born to two people who survived the Holocaust: "My family life was very, very bleak for the most part – defined by my mother's unending grief and my father's nightmares." Rosalie constantly sought liberation from her dark depression until, after a spell of terrible psychic pain, she came face to face with an extraordinary healing opportunity that deeply affected her life direction. She saw an advertisement that said, "Children of survivors of the Holocaust wanted to meet with children of Nazis." In her words, this is what followed:

I went to Germany and sat in one of the most sacred circles I have ever been in… a circle of descendants of the Third Reich face to face with descendants of Jewish and Christian victims and survivors. We each told our story and we saw that everyone there was in pain. These horrible crimes had not just happened to the victims' side, they also pervaded the psyches of those on the other side because these people felt such horrible feelings of guilt and shame.

And so, after four days of listening to and telling the untold stories of the Holocaust and the culture of Nazism, and feeling heard, we saw this release start to happen and we felt we had taken our heaviest burdens off our shoulders. Those people did more for me, and I assume we did for them, than years of therapy because they validated our experience. The Germans' apologies set us free, "I'm so sorry for what my people did to your people" were words that unlocked the vaults of pain for those on the side of the victims. The victims' words, "You are not responsible for what our parents did, only for what you do" unfastened the shackles of those on the perpetrators' side. We experienced a transformation, both individually and collectively. And, it was Otto, the man I had feared most, who kissed my forehead and gave me his heartfelt apologies when my turn came to share the tragedies of my family. His sincerity released something in me that had been held shut for a lifetime.

Extract from *Mourning Has Broken* by Carmella B'Hahn.[33]

* The Practice *

Moons in Moccasins

Read the Curiosity Step, then do the Curiosity Chair exercise, if you are holding challenging feelings about anyone's behaviour. If not, do it later or repeat it any time you feel at odds with anyone this week.

The Curiosity Step

This empathy skill has only one step… into curiosity. You need only the willingness and ability to be curious. With curiosity, even the most entrenched positions can move to an inclusive stance where the other person can feel fully respected.

Disarm your "opponent" when in an argument, or when different opinions are bouncing back and forth, by stepping into genuine interest, "I'm curious to know why you have come to that conclusion. Tell me more about… so I can understand." Throw yourself into discovering what it's like experiencing the issue from their position.

Curiosity Chair Exercise[34]

(Use when you have recurring, strong thoughts/emotions about someone.)

+ Firstly, vividly imagine this person sitting in a chair near you. Recall the details about their way of being that is disturbing you. Then say to them out loud or silently, "I am curious about your experience".
+ Next, move and sit in the chair you imagined them in and see how far you can intuit their viewpoint. What is it like to be them in this situation? What are their feelings/beliefs? Allow impressions to arise in answer to your desire to know how it is for them.
+ Change chairs again and think on how you might behave differently with them when you meet them?

During "Moons in Moccasins" Week

Simply use the Curiosity Step as often as you can when you find yourself disagreeing with someone else's view or behaviour – including people in the media… "I wonder what leads them to think/be that way"? Discover what happens and make notes of what worked.

Supportive Resource: *The Believing Game*, Peter Elbow.[35]

WEEK 27

Savouring Successes

Noticing how far we've come
(The half-way point)

> ## * Opportunity *
>
> To bolster our awareness of what is now
> working well in our relationships with
> self, life and others.

*People who live the most fulfilling lives
are the ones who are
always rejoicing at what they have.*

~ RICHARD CARLSON
(Author and Psychotherapist)

This week is different. If you have been following the chapters systematically, you will have covered 26 aspects of relating. Now it's time to pause, to integrate what you've taken in – by whatever learning style you chose – and to take a week off any new input.

There is a temptation when facing new learning to focus on what isn't right – what is missing, rather than what has been found. This week is about allowing awareness to surface of all that *is* working.

Cast your eyes *lightly* on the list below to jog your memory (this is not a test). What has had the most constructive effect on the way you relate and is now part of your natural language and behaviour repertoire? Look back through your journal for earlier insights. If need be, keep bringing yourself back to what *is* working now.

Covered in the first half of Heart of Relating

1. Awakening the Body
2. Oh, Yes I Can!
3. Look Who's Talking!
4. In the Zone
5. Watching the Match
6. Inner Talk
7. Ego Watch
8. Who's Driving?
9. Speak for Yourself
10. Love Without Falling
11. I'm All Ears!
12. Wounds Listen
13. Joining the Dots
14. The Judge's Pendulum
15. Going Into Space
16. My Media Message
17. Juicy Gossip
18. Larger than Life
19. Time Travelling
20. Who Said That?
21. Thought-Bodies
22. Please, Please Me
23. The Real Deal
24. Clear as a Bell
25. Heart and Head Weave
26. Moons in Moccasins

During "Savouring Successes" Week
Whether in a partnership/group or not, do the following:

 • Talk with someone about the constructive changes you have seen in yourself (and others if applicable) and what you use most from what you have learned.

 • Refer to the paradigm model at the beginning of the book and look at where you stand now. In what ways has your understanding of relating from the inside out expanded?

Are the sounds you hear right now
inside or outside you?
You can think *that they are "outside",*
but in your actual direct experience,
if you listen openly, is there a boundary?
Can you find the place where "inside" becomes
"outside" and visa versa?
Is there anything outside
or separate from awareness?
Is there a "you" apart from
or other than awareness itself? [36]

~ JOAN TOLLIFSON
(Author)

*Instead of assuming matter
to be the primary reality,
we need to turn our model of reality
inside out
and put consciousness firmly
at the centre of things.*

~PETER RUSSELL
(Author and Physicist)

WEEK 28
I think I'll Feel

Finding the guidance of our felt sense

---

* Opportunity *

To prevent thinking ourselves into emotional
states by listening instead to our
felt sense/innate guidance system.

---

*Emotions are created by your thoughts, particularly
unquestioned judgements about yourself or others.
In contrast, feelings are an essential and intelligent
way of knowing that connects you to yourself, others
and your environment in simple
and at times profound ways.*

~ RICHARD MOSS
(Author and Conscious Living Teacher)

PLEASE NOTE

*Getting caught up in the semantics of the words "emotions"
and "feelings" will deflect you from learning.
The dictionary does not have the perfect words to choose from.
Simply stay open to testing out the definition above.*

I t is time to expand on a central theme that weaves through almost every section of *Heart of Relating* and deeply affects our interactions: our relationship with our thoughts and the emotions they create.

In "Awakening the Body" we explored the difference between the head position of *thinking about,* where we label and distance ourselves from what consider as "other", and the sensory position of *being with* where we feel our connection. In "Look Who's Talking" we looked at how we tend to identify with our thoughts as if they *are* us, and we considered a bigger sense of Self beyond thought. In "Inner Talk" we saw how we affect our self-esteem by turning our thoughts on ourselves, and in "Joining the Dots" we experienced how we think up fictional stories to fill in the gaps rather than checking facts. In "Who's Driving?" we covered how we can be in the passenger seat or driving seat of our thoughts to create our experience of life. In "Time Travelling" we touched on how our thoughts absent us from the present into past and future and create emotions such as guilt, sadness, worry, fear and anticipation.

Conscious Living Teacher, Richard Moss (as well as Eckhart Tolle), emphasises the importance of understanding the difference between emotions generated by thought and what he calls feelings, which are natural, instinctual expressions of the human organism. See previous quote.

Emotions are useful as signals to highlight our thought processes and beliefs so that we can share and change them if we choose. However, once we stop seeing our thoughts, beliefs and judgements as a large part of our identity (Week 3), *body-centred* feelings have space to arise naturally and our thoughts will be freed to create constructively.

FEELINGS ARE LIKE AN INNATE GUIDANCE SYSTEM WITH WHICH TO SENSE THE WORLD DIRECTLY.

Feelings range from a sense of heaviness and grief to lightness, gratitude, joy and bliss. They are a passing state of being that will move through of its own accord when ready – like clouds. Emotions will stay as long as we continue the thoughts that create them.

Story Time

The Gifts of Pain

For two weeks I was suffering excruciating nerve pain in my teeth and into my ear. Neither dentist nor doctor was able to locate a clear physical cause and so I used this challenging opportunity to watch how my thoughts affected the physical pain and to differentiate between mind-made emotions and natural feelings.

My tears have always poured as a physiological response to pain, but finally, I have learned to tell when I add emotion to the natural flow by allowing "poor-me" types of thoughts to flood in. With this nerve pain, I could see that the extra pressure of my thought-made emotions made it near impossible to make decisions about how to act – what medication to take, who to call, etc. My emotions were swamping and debilitating my logical thought.

I would describe the following as my natural feelings: *shock* from the waves of searing pain with deep *peace* in-between; *exhaustion* from lack of sleep; *hunger; compassion* for others in physical pain and *gratitude* for the health I've taken for granted.

Following are added thoughts and consequent mind-made reactions:
What if the pain doesn't end soon? – caused panic.
I can't control the pain – led to helplessness and fear.
I need to sleep so I can work – brought anxiety, not sleep.
This is unbearable – created physical tension and contraction.
It will improve tomorrow – caused hope then shock when it worsened.

I believe I have an intelligent body-wisdom that guides me, given the chance. During the pain onslaught, I was at times deaf to this guidance, listening instead to the emotional voices shouting for relief of symptoms, and feeding them with painkillers. At other times, I listened to the quieter voice of guidance, which asked for drug-free spells to enable underlying anxieties and psychological causes to make themselves known. When allowing the feelings of pain, I found new awareness surfacing about my inability to speak as a child, allowing me to release a behaviour pattern that was literally crying out for attention. The pain was gone soon after.

✻ The Practice ✻

I Think I'll Feel

Read this passage from *A New Earth* by Eckhart Tolle.[37]

> *Positive emotions generated by the ego already contain within themselves their opposite into which they can quickly turn…*
>
> *What the ego calls love is possessiveness and addictive clinging that can turn into hate within a second. Anticipation about an upcoming event, which is the ego's evaluation of future, easily turns into its opposite – let-down and disappointment – when the event is over or doesn't fill the ego's expectation…*
>
> *Emotions exist within the realm of opposites.*
>
> *States of Being [felt sense] can be obscured but they have no opposite. They emanate from within you as the love, joy and peace that are aspects of your true nature.*

Note in your journal the impact of these words. Sense for a moment your emotional life to date and the opposites it has contained.

During "I Think I'll Feel" Week

Keep your journal with you to make notes. This week is about learning to differentiate between your thought-made emotions and natural feelings/body wisdom. Whenever you observe yourself going off into any thought or story that is causing emotion, either "positive" or "negative", bring yourself back to direct, *felt* experience. Move from your head to your body's sensory guidance:

- ◆ What is the actual sensation in my body now?
- ◆ What does my gut feeling or intuition express when I drop thinking, analysing and making meaning and *sit with* whatever is occurring?

At the end of the week, as always, note what struck you as important and any changes you are choosing to make.

Please Note: Trauma – being flooded by strong emotion where something deeper than present thought is affecting you – could need professional help. Is now the time to give yourself that support?

Supportive Resources: *A New Earth*, Eckhart Tolle.[38]
Inside-Out Healing, Dr Richard Moss.[39]

Bird's Eye View

Seeing the bigger picture

> ### * Opportunity *
>
> To expand our compassion and sense of connection by noticing the wider context and network of which we are all a part.

*The
eyes
experience
less stress
when they can look upon a wider horizon.*

~ R. D. CHIN
(Feng Shui Architect)

*S*taying connected with our felt sense and our own perspective, *at the same time* as moving in and out of various other "viewpoints" as we relate, is a communication art that enriches relationships. This is as if we are a tree *as well as* the bird that is nesting in it. The bird can fly to someone else's tree nearby (from which it can experience that viewpoint and see its own nest and how its chicks are doing) and it can soar skyward to take in the panoramic view whenever it wants to.

When we learn to move our awareness from our own skin (or tree) into another's experience as we are interacting – as seen in Moons in Moccasins – Week 26, we become aware of their needs and viewpoint, as well as noticing new things about our own behaviour and communication. This is useful as it opens our eyes to the context.

AWARENESS OF THE CONTEXT OF INTERACTIONS IS KEY.

Everything ever communicated rests in a context that is easy to miss when we are focussed intently on the topic at hand. Selfishness and blame arise from a narrow viewpoint, but from a wider perspective we can take into account what kind of morning, day, week, life, each have had. We can expand our view to reach far beyond the words exchanged, to include: health; age and life experience (or lack of it); history with each other and the topic; possible wounds being triggered. From a wider perspective, compassion is often evoked and a desire to meet everyone's best interest can naturally arise.

Certain interactions or happenings make no sense at all without us finding a "bird in the sky" overview that is more expansive than our own or another's viewpoint. Below is an example of two ways I can relate to my son's death: from a personal viewpoint (a); and a wider perspective (b), which I explain further in my Perspective Heals story.

    a) I am a mother whose son has drowned and that feels excruciating.
    b) Leaves fall from the trees at different times. Not everyone lives till they are old. Death is a natural part of life.

Neither viewpoint is wrong. Holding them together can be helpful, and in this example, the wider perspective soothes the personal one.

Story Time

Perspective Heals

When my son died, my sanity was saved by my learned ability to dance between different perspectives. Had I identified solely with the mother in me whose child had drowned in a shocking river incident (1st position), I think I would have broken down, and my ability to relate well with loved ones who were also in mourning would have been nil. During that agonising time, I questioned others about their experiences of his death (2nd position) as well as seeking the wider perspective that asked the bigger questions about death itself (3rd position). Consequently, the patchwork of experiences became an extraordinary quilt when pieced together:

> Benjaya was a water baby who came into and out of life through water. His blessing song, sung to him at six months old, goes:
> *The river is flowing... down to the sea, mother earth carry me, a child I will always be, mother earth carry me back to the sea.*
>
> The week before he died he said, "Don't get your hopes up, mum, I'm not going up to the next class" and, "When I die, will you be sad and will I see your old cat?" He gave away his precious toys, made a skull and cross-bone flag and played drowning his Lego pirates in a blue ribbon river. Meanwhile, miles away, his small friend played drowning his toys repeatedly. At the same time, in India, Benjaya's cousin, Sommer, played drowning herself in a pool and asked my mother, "Who would you rather have die, Carmella or Benjaya?" Later, when swimming in the sea, a wild dog died in the waves beside them, and, soon after, they were informed of Benjaya's water death by a man called "Jaya".

Having opened to these aspects of the wider story, I could not see my son's death as a tragic accident. An accident is something unforeseen, but his death *was* foreseen. Lifting my awareness to what existed beyond my own emotional trauma enabled me to see synchronicities that tapped me into a network of interconnected human experience and allowed comfort and support to flow in. This opened me to the possibility that Benjaya's death was a perfectly orchestrated finale.[40]

* The Practice *

Bird's Eye View

Three Bird Positions

1st (bird in my tree): Focussing on my own needs.
2nd (bird in someone else's tree): Empathising with the needs of others.
3rd (bird flying high): Observing myself/life from a distance and taking the much wider context into account.

In your journal answer:

◆ Do I have a tendency to live in one of these three positions more than another? If so, which one?

Write as much as you like about you and the Three Bird Positions.

During "Bird's Eye View" Week

Keep checking in with yourself about which position you are in and how the balance feels between self, other and the bigger picture. (You might find you are flitting to all three.)

Example: My daughter is going on a school camping trip and I know heavy rain is forecast. Here are three possible responses:

1st position: Imagining the mountains of washing I will be doing.
2nd position: Concerned about the effect of the rain on my daughter's experience because she has a cold. Give her honey and lemon to take.
3rd position: Imagining the group bonding that's possible when things are tough. Send enough lemons and honey for everyone.

Especially look out for opportunities to move to a wider viewpoint, such as when feeling judgemental and/or challenged by someone's behaviour.
Can you reach a place that thinks, "I wonder why s/he's being like this today?" or, "There must be a bigger picture here that I don't know about."

What is the learning this week on which you will act in future?

Supportive Resource: Neuro Linguistic Programming (NLP).[41]

WEEK 30

Lost in Translation

Choosing well in the electronic world

> ## * Opportunity *
>
> To become conscious of the effects of
> using electronic communication and to
> make choices that work well.

*Children coming forth today have a greater capacity to deal with the greater
variety of information that is coming forward than you did...
This generation gap that you are talking about,
it has ever been thus. Each new generation,
every new individual, that comes forth,
is coming with you having prepared a different platform
for them to proceed from.
There is this thing that gets in the way of that
that says, "I'm the parent. I got here first.
I know more than you do."
From the children's perspective...
what they are saying is,
"You're the parent. You got here first.
You prepared a platform that I am leaping off from –
and my leap will be beyond anything
that you have ever known."*

~ ABRAHAM-HICKS[42]
(Wisdom Teachers)

There is a massive communication and lifestyle difference between those who use technology, social media and texting, and those who don't. In my humble opinion (IMHO), relationships – particularly across the generations – will suffer if bridges are not built. Elders have decades of life learning to pass on, and many youngsters have "techno savvy" which they could, if willing and welcome, "reverse mentor" to those who are open to it.

My grandmother, Esther, called the street "the horse road", put clothes through a mangle, sang from sheet music around the piano, wrote letters in ink and spoke to people in the flesh using her mouth. Acronyms? She might have used SWALK, ASAP and PTO but little else.

In his late teens, my son, Asher, was rarely separated from his "do-everything" Smartphone, iPod, earphones or laptop. He "spoke" with his fingers – globally, had never heard of a horse road or mangle and never bought an envelope or stamp… although he did learn to write with a pen. Once, when I entered his room to ask a question, he said, "You can't just talk to me!" He meant that he couldn't hear with his earphones in, but these words symbolised something to me about the prevalent and growing trend in communication.

He went on to say, "I'm not lost in electronic gadgets, you know. I can concentrate on many things at once and I *can* stop whatever I'm doing to speak to you. I don't think I want to speak to adults any less than previous generations that didn't have earphones or screens – I just have a more obvious way of avoiding it! I know it can be hurtful if I choose not to speak, but at least I'm being honest. With mates (M8s) we just nudge each other when we want to speak, we don't assume friends are unavailable and get cross about their 'absence'."

Global electronic interactions – downloading information/music, social networking, and fingertip communication – will no doubt continue to develop in their own speedy way. I suggest we
KEEP CALM AND KEEP UP
as best we can, remaining conscious of the ways it both helps and hinders our communication patterns.

Translations of Text and Chat Lingo
FYI (For your information)

LOL: Laughing out loud (used to be Lots of love)
OMG: Oh my God! (now used verbally too)
TYVM: Thank you very much, **TY or THX**: Thanks
2moro: Tomorrow
2nite: Tonight
BTW: By the way
PEEPS or PPL: People
BRB: Be right back (used in instant messaging)
PLS: Please
WBU: What about you?
TXT: Text
CM: Call me
IDK: I don't know
L8R: Later
NP: No problem
RU?: Are you?
MSG: Message
B4: Before
NE1: Anyone
GR8: Great
ILY: I love you
XOXO: Hugs and kisses
B4N: Bye for now
:) Happy   :(Sad   :D Laughing

Communication devices constantly evolve, as does the lingo we use when tapping in our messages. It can be hard to keep up! Our overused texting thumbs on phones needed help from shortcuts to gain speed, and now (as well as abbreviations) using quicker-to-type lowercase letters with minimal punctuation is normal. The style used on phones has now spilled into use on other larger devices that *do* have keyboards, making it inevitable (even if we don't text…yet), that we will have to open to this new language if we want to engage with its users.

* The Practice *

Lost in Translation

If you *do* use electronic communication devices
Answer the following three questions in your journal:

  ◆ How does my use of electronic communication (e-mail, Skype, social networking, texting, etc.) benefit my ability to relate?

E.g.: I connect more than ever with others – next door or across the world; receive e-mails about social events and meet more people; listen to fascinating teachings about relationships on the Internet.

  ◆ How is my electronic communication detrimental to my inter-personal connections?

E.g.: Hours on-line means less face-to-face contact; staring at a screen affects my mood and health; my phone is a distraction and (OMG!) an addiction; I'm not fully present with those in front of me.

  ◆ What changes in my habits would be useful?

E.g.: Slow down and take breaks; remember how easy it is to misinterpret words without any tonal inflection, body language, etc.; clearly indicate my feelings; don't take my phone to...

If you *don't*, or rarely, use electronic devices to communicate
Brainstorm about both the benefits and detrimental effects of not relating via electronic channels and capture any constructive actions you choose to take.

During "Lost in Translation" Week
Put into action any ideas for constructive change that have arisen and initiate a conversation about anything that has come up for you on this topic with others.

Is there anyone who doesn't use the same communication medium with whom it might be useful to build a bridge? How will you do it?

Report the results in your journal. What will you keep up doing?

Supportive Resource: *Computer-Mediated Communication In Personal Relationships*, Kevin B. Wright and Lynne M. Webb.[43]

Bows and Arrows

Balancing the masculine and feminine

* Opportunity *

To get where we want or need to be in a
balanced way by allowing intuition
to inform our action.

Be like the bow and arrow…
one cannot be fulfilled without the other.
Each gives purpose to the other.
Without the bow the arrow cannot fly.
Without the arrow the bow is empty.

~ JOSEPH M. MARSHALL III
(Lakota Historian and Writer)

The shape of a bow is curved like the new moon, like archetypal feminine energy. It is the strong, holding base in which the arrow is received and centred before its purposeful release. An arrow that flies true from the bow is straight and aimed at a target, as masculine energy is naturally drawn to do. Together they serve their purpose.

Whether male or female, every human is a meld of feminine and masculine energies, and the ratio we each hold of these energies is fundamental to the way we relate. Balancing our own inner feminine and masculine is the name of the game, especially if we want to avoid co-dependence. In co-dependent communication we are dependent on others to help us relate, e.g. letting another speak for us or speaking on their behalf when there is no need to do so.

The western world has been dominated by a primarily masculine mode of communication for a long time. Generally speaking, both sexes are now well skilled in the art of *doing* and "outside-in" relating. We tend to move fast like the arrow; we plan and steer our lives towards our goals for the future. We gather information from outside ourselves and use our reasoning power to fix and work things out, to debate and form opinions. We live and work mostly in angular buildings and often sit in straight lines in public places. None of this is wrong, but I'm left questioning: How many of our arrows have lost sight of the bow and how can we reunite them?

THE FEMININE FEELS SAFE AND TRUSTING IN THE
UNKNOWN AND SEES THIS EMPTINESS
AS A BIRTHING PLACE FOR ACTION.

The way of the bow, the true feminine energy, is the way of *being*; of patient, deep listening to intuition; of sensing feelings; of surrender and just knowing. This "inside-out" way values non-action, takes time and space (as covered in "Going Into Space") and it trusts an arrow-like direction to emerge when necessary from this beingness. The feminine creates soft, supporting, curved environments that nourish, and it knows how to sit with apparent brokenness to await solutions from within, moving only when the impulse strikes.

Story Time

Giving Birth from a Listening Womb

During my first pregnancy in 1986, my partner, Abel, and I researched and tuned in to what felt ideal for the coming birth. We planned a home water birth without drugs, in a womb-like, candlelit attic room with loved ones supporting us. We recognised the baby's safety as paramount and agreed to go willingly to hospital if need be. It was to be the first ever water birth in the Midlands of England, which health authorities were planning to thwart due to their fear of the unknown nature of this new way of birth.

At a routine doctor's check-up, 10 days before my due date, I had a small "show" of blood – normal for the onset of labour. The doctor spoke of the possibility of haemorrhaging and bundled me into an ambulance bound for the nearest hospital. There, I was transferred to a coverless bed by wheelchair, dressed in a gaping blue smock and connected to a foetal monitor and glucose drip. Surrounded by an air of clinical authority, certainty of my ignorance, and assumed control, I felt my voice and my power ebbing away. I longed for someone to stop, to connect with me, look at me, and LISTEN to what I felt.

Eventually, Abel and my mother arrived, and together we set about making a balanced response to this turn of events. We discovered the facts: I was in early labour with no complications and I could legally discharge myself and continue my birth plans at home. Our impulse was to leave on the spot, and yet we wanted be sure that this was a wise move and not simply a reaction to the uncomfortable environment. What if there was an unseen reason why I had been brought to the hospital? So we closed the door and sat in silence, communally sensing whether we felt any danger lurking beyond our conscious awareness. We all three felt a green light and a sense of trust. So, I signed the discharge papers with a flourish and skipped jubilantly out of hospital to give birth to my son, Benjaya, at home, in candlelit water, without drugs and surrounded by love.

Read the whole story in *Benjaya's Gifts*.[44]

* The Practice *

Bows and Arrows

Imagine holding a bow and arrow and feeling the relationship between the two as you draw back the straight arrow right into the curve of the bow before you take aim. Imagine the difference – in terms of reaching the target – between doing this in a hurry and doing it slowly and steadily using all your senses to feel the perfect tension before release.

Walk of the Bow – 10/15 min exercise

Do this as soon as you can take relaxed time to be outside. It is a walk to help embody the way of the bow, and to bring into consciousness how much can be missed when striding towards a goal.

> Stand at your door *without thought of destination* and allow something outside to catch your attention. Move towards this *slowly*, listening to and feeling each of your steps on the ground. Stay with your focus in open curiosity for as long as it retains your interest, being alert to any metaphors that it might reflect about yourself, e.g. this bush needs watering... do I drink enough water? Continue the walk by letting your intuition guide you on, trusting an experience to unfold rather than you being the director.

Return after 10/15 min and draw/write any insights in your journal.

During "Bows and Arrows" Week

Objectively observe your communication for the balance you hold of the masculine (doing) and feminine (being). Reread the previous two pages as a reminder, if necessary. Write about this in your journal. See if any ideas arise as to how to bring about more balance. For instance, it might benefit you to stop for a moment when you hear yourself giving a list of reasons for doing something and ask, "What is my gut feeling about this?" Alternatively, if you tend to get lost in your feelings, you could pause and ask yourself, "What is the purpose of this conversation and what facts would be useful to clarify?"

Supportive Resource: *Walking With Grandfather, The Wisdom of Lakota Elders,* Joseph M. Marshall III.[45]

WEEK 32

Space Invaders

Attending to our own business

---

* Opportunity *

To increase our available energy by tending to
our own business and allowing others
to learn for themselves.

---

*Never miss an opportunity
to make others happy,
even if you have to leave them alone
in order to do it.
Specially if you have to leave them alone!*

~ AUTHOR UNKNOWN

Question
Whose business are you in?

~ BYRON KATIE
(Author and Self-awareness Facilitator)

How much of our time and energy would be freed if we kept out of other people's business and dropped our "shoulds" and "shouldn'ts"? The well-being of those who truly cannot stand on their own feet in the world *is* the business of those who can, but it is not our business to worry about and to offer unsolicited advice and help to those who could look after themselves if we let them. How often do we feel our space being invaded and our room to think and feel for ourselves filled by another's opinion and desire to convince or assist?

I have a friend who used to innocently dampen my pleasure of shopping in the belief that she was helping. She scouted for what I needed, suggested options, and left me responding to her ideas rather than leaving me free to enjoy the hunt and discovery for myself.

Do you recognize the plaintive or self-righteous voice of self or other saying, "I'm only trying to help!" and the communication knots that ensue when we think we are being kind but aren't? Others' well-intentioned help can sap our energy – especially if we want to decline it. Remember the story of "Giving or Giving In?" – Week 22? How often do we give in and accept help or advice that we don't want?

IT FEELS EMPOWERING TO LEARN BY THE DIRECT
EXPERIENCE OF OUR OWN EFFORTS.

We can hinder another's learning by erasing their opportunity to learn directly, even if we do know more or could do it better. As long as I reminded my son repeatedly to do his homework, he was reliant on my nagging. The difficult alternative – school detention, was a far better teacher! This withdrawal of thinking for others, which will allow their autonomy, can be challenging, but also transformational for relationships – especially with young people.

Suggestions
   ◆ Ask yourself often, "Whose business am I in?"
   ◆ Check if your offering would be welcome.
   ◆ If you feel invaded, say so!
   E.g. I appreciate your caring but I need to do this for myself.

Story Time

Consulting the Unbiased Few

In Heart and Head Weave – Week 25, I told one aspect of the story about the momentous decision-making needed when my son's father, Abel, asked if Asher could go and live with him in China. Here is another aspect, which speaks to this Space Invaders theme.

To set the scene: Asher was adamant he didn't want to go to Shanghai because he was petrified of the change, which brought up the issue of his rights. He was frightened of even small changes at that time. His father and stepmother were offering him the best education that money could buy. However, because of practicalities, I would only be able to see Asher twice a year at the most. Tough for one whose first son had died. Abel had promised to give Asher the love he had not managed to give his brother, and he especially wanted to support him through his transition into manhood.

Word of my challenge spread fast and I was soon thrown off-balance by the surge of invasion I felt by friends who thought they were rallying to my support. Those who imagined my emotional pain or feared losing their own children said it was an outrageous request and were incensed; men who missed their own father's parenting were adamant that a boy needs his father at that age; others felt the need to fight Asher's corner so that he could stay if that's what he wanted. On and on went the different opinions and advice as to what I *should* do.

I soon stopped speaking of the situation to anyone except an unbiased few, and listened deeply to those who would be directly affected by the decision. I thanked others for their passion to help and asked them to trust that my decision would be based on what I felt resonated with me as the best way forward, however difficult living with that decision might prove to be. Then, in the relative stillness, free of opinions, it became clear – "yes, I will let him go".

Five years later, I had a moment of utter satisfaction as I heard Asher telling someone who had spoken out for his right to stay, how much he valued his international education and that he believed I had made the decision that was in his best interest.

✳ The Practice ✳

Space Invaders

Answer in your journal:
- ◆ Who is the main invader of my space?

Allow a memory to arise of a time when you felt someone was stepping too far into your business. Feel the effect that this had on your body and recall your reaction – whether or not it was verbalised, e.g. I felt myself contract and wanted to pull away physically, my unspoken words were, "Get off my back and let me handle it."

Now consider:
- ◆ Whose space do I invade?

Invite a memory to surface of when you stepped into someone else's business. How did this feel in your body and what else was happening for you? E.g. I couldn't bear the tension and stress of trying to hold back my advice, so gave it in a tone that expected rejection. When I wasn't received, I felt like shouting, "Why can't you value my experience?"

Write about this incident with as much detail as you can remember.

Answer two more questions:
- ◆ What will I choose to do differently when I feel as if someone is invading my space?
- ◆ How might I respond more constructively when I am tempted to invade someone else's space?

During "Space Invaders" Week

1. Apply any learning from above about who invades your space, whose space you invade and what you might do differently.

2. Reread and use, whenever appropriate, the three important suggestions listed earlier (at the bottom of the page).

3. Turn the spotlight on your motivation for helping others and ask:
- ◆ Do I need to apply the help I am offering others, to myself?

Note down what has made the most impression on you this week regarding the invasion of personal space.

Mirror, Mirror...

Seeing our own reflection in others

> ## * Opportunity *
>
> To shed light on our inner shadows by seeing each person as a mirror in which something about ourselves is reflected.

*We don't see things as they are,
we see them as we are.*

~ ANAIS NIN
(Author)

> ## TIP FROM HR STUDY GROUP
>
> *Is your will still behind doing this work?*
> *If not, take a break and align your will.*
> *Give yourself the choice when or whether to continue.*
> *What would work for you?*

We live in a house of mirrors; every being we meet offering a particular reflection of ourselves. But do we dare to look in these human mirrors and learn from the useful reflections? Most of us have been taught, by the example of others, to blame anyone whose behaviour disturbs our status quo. This results in us pushing away our most revealing mirrors – our finest teachers. Blaming prevents us from having to face our own shadows. We could ask instead:

WHAT COULD I POLISH IN MYSELF WHEN I RECOGNISE IT IN THE MIRROR OF ANOTHER'S BEHAVIOUR?

We unconsciously project that which is hidden or disowned in ourselves onto others, and this can cause enormous confusion.

Examples of Projection

1. Lynne has a problem making her voice heard and therefore dislikes and is frustrated by anyone who verbally takes up a lot of space. Unconsciously, she makes them the *cause* of her "disability" rather than a *reminder* of it and thinks *they* should change their behaviour.

2. Mark meets Joe – a man whose critical streak stirs memories of his abusive father. He is triggered into feeling disempowered, angry and emotionally absent in Joe's presence and over-reacts, assuming that Joe's behaviour is causing his intense feelings. Mark dislikes Joe and blurts out his negative opinion of him to others. There is a grain of truth here: Joe's critical streak, onto which the projection has been stuck. This is also called "transference" in the psychology world. Mark has transferred his critical father's image onto Joe.

Those projected upon are likely to feel bewildered by the exaggerated judgements of their behaviour, although they might recognise some truth in what's being said. To become the screen for a projection, there has to be something that triggers it.

We see others through our mental filters, and what we see differs according to how clean our lenses are. Although our best friends are fabulous at mirroring parts of ourselves we like, painful but very useful blessings are mirrored by those whose behaviour we detest.

Story Time

As Within: So Without

Long ago, I facilitated a weekend workshop entitled "As Within: So Without" with my mother, M'haletta. We were seeking to expand our understanding of Universal Law and were curious about how much we can discover about ourselves by examining our immediate external world and our perceptions of it.

We led an exercise – a silent walk in the picturesque Clent Hills of the English Midlands, instructing participants to pay close attention to what they noticed on their walk. What an eye-opener it was! Later, when we asked them to describe their walks, not one person had a similar experience, despite walking the same path.

I vividly remember one agitated woman, who on return, angrily shared about the amount of litter that she had encountered on her walk. "I cannot believe how people can take so little responsibility for their rubbish," she ranted. She had started picking it up and finally gave up in disgust. No one else had been disturbed by or had particularly noticed the litter that obviously did exist.

Given time to reflect on why she might have honed in on the litter when others hadn't, she remembered that one of her parents had been obsessive about cleanliness and the other had been prone to seeing the negative side of everything. This was an "ah ha!" moment for her as she saw that her whole view of the world and people in it was tainted by the shadows of her parents' behaviour on her lens. In her life she was frustrated and exhausted by trying to clear up what she saw as other people's mess at the same time as tightly hiding her own perceived imperfections. This could now change.

Later she went out on a second walk, intending to accept the litter as best she could and to see how much beauty she could let in to her experience. She noticed the breath-taking view for the first time.

> *The "Mirroring the Gold" exercise – coming up – is based on one created by Paul Solomon (Inner Light Consciousness) in 1981. Byron Katie offers similar, more in-depth teaching called "The Work".*

* The Practice *

Mirror, Mirror…

Projecting: We judge a trait in another as unacceptable/negative and make them responsible for our emotional reaction, when it is really triggering something about ourselves that we haven't yet seen.

Firstly, prepare your journal, as suggested below, for the Mirroring exercise and practise now on a past or live situation. **During the week,** and for as long as it proves fruitful, keep filling in the columns when you find yourself triggered and blaming.

Mirroring the Gold Exercise
On a double-page spread, write the following on the left-hand page:

THE MIRROR

<u>Incident Name</u>	<u>What I don't like</u>	<u>I want you to realise…</u>

Whenever you feel emotionally triggered by anyone, name the incident/emotion, e.g. "Burned pie anger". Next, *imagine* pointing your finger and, *without holding back*, telling them what you don't like about them or what they do/did. Write the essence of this in column 2. Now imagine telling them what you want them to realise about themselves, and capture this in a nutshell in column 3.

Your right-hand page will look like this:

THE GOLD

<u>True of me?</u>	<u>What *I* realise about me</u>	<u>I'm grateful for…</u>

You are now looking for the gold in the mirror of this incident i.e., realisation of what needs bringing to light in *you*. First, scan your past for memories of similar feelings or incidents and stay open to the idea that something in you might be attracting this dynamic.

Now ask yourself the following and fill in the columns:
  ◆ How is what I don't like about them, also true of me?
  ◆ What can I learn about my behaviour from this?
  ◆ What am I grateful for from this incident?

If you find any projections you want to take back, think about making an apology (see Week 42) or thanking the person concerned.

WEEK 34

It's Contagious!

Becoming positively infectious

> ## * Opportunity *
>
> To become conscious of, and therefore able to choose, what we are spreading or absorbing in our daily relating.

Even among complete strangers,
a moment of playfulness,
even outright silliness
forms an instant resonance.

~ DANIEL GOLEMAN
(Author and Psychologist)

Our state of being is highly contagious! Neuroscientists show how inter-connected brain cells, called mirror neurons, automatically and instantaneously copy and download others' facial expressions, movements and emotions onto our own neurons, allowing us to experience others as if from inside them. Giacomo Rizzolatti, who discovered mirror neurons, said, "These systems allow us to grasp the minds of others not through conceptual reasoning but through direct simulation; by feeling not by thinking."[46]

Cinema-goers en masse synch their mood changes to the tone of the movie scenes, and swathes of sports supporters do likewise according to their team's play.

WE CATCH THE PREDOMINANT MOOD
UNLESS OUR OWN INNER STATE IS STRONGER.

In a situation such as being surrounded by 2,000 dismayed football fans, or even being with one angry or depressed person, staying in our own mood is a tall order for most people. If we have been on automatic pilot all day, the answer to, "What was your day like?" will be based on our emotional interactions with all the characters, real or fictional (on TV/theatre, etc.), we have encountered since waking.

Social skills, especially rapport and empathy, are created and refined by this ability to absorb another's state, but can we let this flow through us and scan for what is useful, rather than becoming affected by it? Successful therapists practise the art of fully receiving and hearing their clients while retaining a strong, balanced state.

I remember once needing to tell a friend something difficult. I was scared because I expected to trigger an angry and rejecting reaction. When preparing what I wanted to say, I had the insight that my tone of fear and negative expectation would most surely spark his anger. And so I focussed on all the things I like about him until I knew my words would come from a genuine state of affection. I also visualised him sensing my care for him and therefore listening and hearing me clearly. It worked – he did exactly this.

Story Time

The Knife's Edge

In another workshop facilitated with my mother, we asked participants to wander around the house or garden to find and bring back an object that could represent how they were feeling. We were aware of strong emotions in the group and wanted to use the power of object symbology to express these without getting embroiled in wordy personal dynamics. Everyone was then invited to lay their object on the cloth in the middle of the room, one by one, and to say a few words about their feelings.

One lovely young man had been stirred by something that morning and was angry. There was tension in the air, which reached a crescendo after he placed his symbol – a large sharp knife from the kitchen – on the cloth. He placed it away from the few other symbols already laid and spoke of his anger and sense of loneliness.

After a long pause, others followed and placed their symbols, all at quite a distance from the knife's edge. This was a powerful and cutting symbol that appeared to be deeply affecting the atmosphere of the room. There was no real physical danger but fear seemed to hang in the air and some of the group were clearly holding their breath.

Thank goodness I felt particularly loving and strong that day. My symbol – a beautiful, open flower head from the garden – was the last to be positioned. As I looked at all the symbols, the gaping space between them and the glinting knife, I saw this man's loneliness played out on the floor. My hand moved and placed the flower directly on his blade. I gently smiled as I looked at him to connect and to check out with a glance if this proximity was acceptable. A brief look of relief passed over his face before he covered it with his hands and wept.

Then, one at a time, everyone moved their objects closer to the knife. The tension broke, fear left and love took its place.

✳ *The Practice* ✳

It's Contagious!

In your journal, answer the following questions:
- ◆ Is there anyone I relate to frequently in whose presence I feel drained? What happens?
- ◆ What is my part in this dynamic? How do I respond?
- ◆ How can I best affect the dynamic by my own behaviour?

Here is a fictional example:

My father criticises me incessantly. I cringe and contract, silently blaming him and wishing I wasn't there. I allow it to happen because I don't speak up and I continue to visit every Sunday. Now, I am choosing to be as "positively" contagious as I can. I will focus on Dad's best qualities before I go, will remind myself who I am and that his criticisms say more about him than me. I will suggest we play Scrabble together and request some fun ideas from him. When he puts me down, I will tell him how drained I've felt by the way he speaks to me and ask how he feels about my visits.

During "It's Contagious" Week

The health of the whole depends on the health of each individual, so this week is about consciously playing a part in our network's health. Every smile or frown we express could be caught by others. Notice what you are spreading and imagine the effect it might be having.

Go out of your way three (or more) times to say something uplifting and out of character… perhaps even to a stranger.

Simply decide to find your way out of any toxic state you feel. If you feel agitated or consumed with difficult emotion, rather than letting it leak out or dumping it on whoever is present, implement a strategy and do something different! Go for a walk, run or jump about; get professional help; do last week's *Mirroring the Gold* exercise; ask permission of someone you trust to splurge it out in a non-PC way… then stop. Rereading In the Zone – Week 4, might help. Only you can make your inner state strong and positively infectious. Note your successes.

Supportive Resource: *Social Intelligence*, Daniel Goleman.[47]

Let's Face It

Taking our heads out of the sand

---

* Opportunity *

To increase our available energy and enhance
relationships, by facing and clearing
sensitive issues as they arise.

---

*In the end,
we will remember
not the words of our enemies
but the silence of our friends.*

~ MARTIN LUTHER KING JR.
(Minister and Civil Rights Activist)

TIP FROM HR STUDY GROUP

*The exercises are tools for everyday living that can be brought
into play when needed. It's not a matter of "done that now!"*

S ilence, withdrawal and turning the other cheek are powerful responses – sometimes needed and perfectly appropriate, and at other times deeply damaging to relationships. It would be helpful to discern the difference and to become conscious of when we are putting our head in the sand as an avoidance strategy.

Someone showing apparent indifference, ignoring us or refusing to acknowledge a problem that we perceive, can incense us. Egos want to be recognised; they want to know they exist. Relating directly with others about sensitive issues – even if it's uncomfortable – gives the message that we both matter; our relationship is worth the effort. Conversely, if we walk away or silently witness something we disagree with, we give the message that it doesn't matter to us. According to a Girl Scouts' website,[48] "when a girl is bullied, 85 percent of the time nobody steps in to help her but more than half the time, when peers speak up, bullying stops within 10 seconds."

WHAT COULD WE PREVENT BY DARING TO SPEAK UP?

Not Facing It (Examples)
1. Being very late or not turning up for an arrangement or delivery without communicating about the change.
2. Owing money but avoiding mentioning it when we can't pay it back on time.
3. Being asked a sensitive question by e-mail and answering all other points mentioned except that one.
4. Walking out of a meeting without explanation.

Facing It
When we face the challenge and sort it to the best of our ability, the energy drain of the avoidance ceases. What works? Summoning our courage and being authentic (see The Real Deal – Week 23), e.g.:

I'm sorry, I've been avoiding talking about returning your money because I am embarrassed. Could you give me another month?; I don't know what to do but I feel uncomfortable hearing this; tell me more about what's going on for you; I'm feeling vulnerable and unclear and need space now; can we speak about this after dinner?

Story Time

Turning Fear Around

When I was seven months pregnant with my first son, I went on a short holiday with friends in a hot mountainous region of southern Spain. One day, three of us went to a nearby lake across a winding mountain path to cool off. It was paradise. There was not a soul about and we swam, sunbathed and picnicked.

The others decided to go back earlier than I was ready, and knowing that it would take me longer to get back up the steep path with my heavy belly, I said I would follow them shortly at my own pace. I watched them stride out of sight, and soon afterwards became aware of a presence nearby and a sense of being watched. Every now and then I saw the foliage move and finally caught sight of a rough-looking, dirty-faced man peering at me intently from behind a bush.

I took some deep breaths, packed up immediately and began to walk as nonchalantly as I could up the path, hand on my womb-child protectively as I went. He followed. I could hear his footsteps getting closer as I slowed down with the effort of the uphill climb. My heart was racing and I recall a powerful feeling of wanting to avoid him at all costs, to get away, get up that hill – anywhere but be in direct contact with this threatening, shady, woman-stalker.

At the point of my greatest fear when the distance between us was narrowing fast, I sent out a loud inner cry for help to the powers that be. The response was instant. I had a memory flash of reading something about the dynamics of being attacked and how if you run, you can encourage both the chase and your victim status. I also remembered that doing something unusual can completely disarm others. And so, with my heart in my mouth, I turned around and perched on an old stone wall to face him as he approached. First I saw his shock, then his fear, as I looked him directly in the eyes. I imagine that in that moment I became a real person to him, pregnant, willing to face him and not to be messed with. Looking disoriented, he nodded his head at me briefly and scuttled on past me up the path. Breathing heavily, I followed *him*.

* The Practice *

Let's Face It

Think about a time when you avoided facing something that you wish you had faced, and the consequences of that inaction. In your journal, write about this and ask yourself specifically:
- How did not facing this affect my emotional and physical state?
- How do I imagine it affected the other party?
- What learning from this can I apply in future?

If we knew we were going to die in two weeks time, we would probably want to deal with our unfinished business with people we care about before then. However long we have left on this earth, we are all on our way towards leaving, so why not start completing some things right now? Imagine a state of being with no loose ends at all, and how free you would feel to engage in the present moment.

Make a list of uneasy places in any of your relationships, however minor – loose ends that might be better addressed or checked out.
Now answer:
- Dealing with which of these would free the most energy in me?

During "Let's Face It" Week
A great deal more energy is probably taken up in the not doing than in the doing itself. Taking into account what feels like "right" timing, set into motion tying up the loose ends that can be addressed now. First, find a way to rest in your strong core (see: In the Zone – Week 4) then make that phone call, apologise, ask clarifying questions, listen to the other person and tell them what is bothering you using "I" statements (examples under the earlier "Facing It" heading).

Be alert to signs of the withdrawal/avoidance dynamic in yourself and others. Practise both giving more of yourself when it might help the situation, and requesting more clarity, e.g. "This is what's happening for me… please tell me your experience of this situation."

Share any successes with someone. Telling your achievement stories can reinforce the lessons learned.

*Communication
keeps passion alive
in relationships.*

~ JOHN GRAY
("Mars and Venus" Author)

Recitation Practice

I have *desires*,
but *I am* not *my desires*.

I can know my desires,
and what can be known
is not the true Knower.

Desires come and go, floating
through my awareness,
but they do not affect
my inward I.

I have *desires* but *I am* not *desires*.

~ KEN WILBER

Feeding the Needy

Responding effectively to neediness

---

* Opportunity *

To gain independence by filling our own needs
where possible and responding appropriately
to others' needs or neediness.

---

*The person who needs
the other person least in a relationship
is the stronger member.*

~ DOUGLAS COUPLAND
(Novelist)

When we communicate clearly what we think we need from a calm inner state (inside-out), the listener will probably be understanding and want to help discover the best course of action to fill that need. On the other hand, needy communication, which comes from a state that longs to be fed and rescued (outside-in), rarely attracts a useful response. When we are needy, we believe that we are not OK unless we are getting what we think we need. Neediness is accompanied by undercurrents such as coercion, a sense of entitlement (I deserve… or others should…) and guilt. It activates co-dependent patterns and often leaves others feeling duty-bound to help, as well as resentful.

Show me a human who doesn't, at times, both exhibit neediness and attempt to rescue others. But, believing we can fix and fill another's emptiness will keep us plugged into a dynamic that will create a "fall" if we ever withdraw our help. This familiar proverb can help:

GIVE A MAN A FISH, FEED HIM FOR A DAY.
TEACH A MAN TO FISH, FEED HIM FOR A LIFETIME.

It is helpful to differentiate between needs and wants because they are often confused. Basic human needs include air, water, food, shelter, warmth and clothing, plus a sense of belonging/love.[49] Strictly speaking, desires for most other things are beliefs about what we think we need to feel satisfied with life – beliefs influenced by our culture, the media's message, our personal history and personality.

Byron Katie says:[50]
Personalities don't love; they want something.
Love doesn't seek anything, it's already complete.
It doesn't want, doesn't need, has no shoulds (not even for the person's own good).

Let's go back to the Identity Model in Week 3 and look at what part of us is speaking when we feel needy – the physical or non-physical identity? Can we shift and strengthen ourselves simply by remembering who we *are* beyond our persona, before letting out a cry for help or attempting to satisfy another's neediness?

Story Time

Whose Need is this?

I once heard a story about a woman (I'll call her Emma) who, in an official capacity, went to see a mother who was experiencing certain challenges in her life. As they talked, this woman's young son was playing happily with a small toy car. Emma was touched to see how much joy he felt from his highly creative games with one little car.

Moved by the troubles of the boy's family, Emma wanted to be helpful. Soon after the visit, when fueling her car, she noticed a national promotion offering, for a certain amount of tokens each, the very toy cars that this young boy loved. So she started collecting tokens and told all her friends to save the tokens until finally she had accumulated a whole array of these toy cars.

Emma went again to call on the family and excitedly presented the young boy with the fruits of her labours. His eyes were wide as he tried to take in the enormity of the gift and he played with them, while again the adults talked.

The next time she visited, the little boy was not playing with any of his cars. She asked him why not and he replied sadly, "because I can't love that many".

Emma's own need to do something good appeared to have swamped this child and even prevented him from continuing to love his one special car.

With thanks to whoever shared this story with me.

PLEASE NOTE
This week's journal work will take a little longer than usual in order to work deeply on our places of neediness.

* The Practice *

Feding the Needy

In your journal, write the word "Needy" in the middle of one page and "Clear Needs" on the one opposite. Now remember how you felt when you were with someone who was expressing neediness, e.g. inadequate, useful, uneasy, claustrophobic. Express these feelings on the "Needy" page using colour and "art" if you like, as well as words.

Now remember being with someone who was clearly stating his/her need. How did you feel? Express this on the other page.

Add words or drawings to both pages that describe how *you* feel when you are needy, and when clearly stating your own needs.

Make a statement to encapsulate anything you learned by doing this.

Taking one close relationship, write out a list of your feelings and needs on a new page, by filling in the dots at least five times.
- ◆ I get upset (angry/irritated, etc.) when s/he... because I need...
E.g. I get upset when *he doesn't verbally appreciate me* because I need *to feel loved* or I get *angry* when she *nags me* because I need *to do things in my way and timing*.

Now imagine standing in your inner strength and write "bonus" by anything listed that feels more like an added bonus than a real need.

Next, identify and put a star by things on the list that feel like important needs to you. (These will be addressed next week.)

Release anything you think is pointless to continue getting upset about, such as: I get upset when he doesn't dance because I need a partner who can dance with me.

During "Feeding the Needy" Week
Whenever you think or use the words, "I need..." check to see if calling it a "want or preference" reduces any feeling of discontent.

Think on and discuss the statement, "Love doesn't seek anything".

Supportive Resource: *I Need Your Love – Is That True*, Byron Katie.[51]

Between You and Me

Talking about unmet needs

* Opportunity *

To experience more happiness as the distress
of unmet needs
is released in self and others.

*When the needs of one person
are being met by the other,
there is laughter.*

~ YAKOV SMIRNOFF
(Comedian)

TIP FROM HR STUDY GROUP

*If you feel overwhelmed by looking at the instructions,
remember that the wider concept is usually easy; it just
needs breaking into small pieces initially, to be understood.*

Unmet needs and wants are the predominant source of unhappiness. Once we have identified our important needs and have released the wants and preferences that we can fulfil for ourselves (see last week), how then do we set about getting those real needs met constructively? Below is one possible way that you will be invited to practise.

The Needs on the Table Exercise (expanded on the Practice Page) looks like this: You will sit with the person you would like to fulfil your unmet needs, with either an imagined or real small table between you. As you speak, you will metaphorically place your needs on the table – the symbolic central place *between you* – to be considered in a balanced and creative way by you both.

When we put issues on the table, we can become more objective. It also highlights how criticisms bypass the table and land on the person, e.g. "You don't listen. I'm sick of banging my head on a wall to be heard" doesn't touch the table. Self-criticism lands on ourself.

The Actual Steps
1. Check your motive. If you don't have *both* people's interest at heart, consider whether or not to proceed.
2. Place your needs on the table for consideration.
3. Stick to facts, avoid conjecture and use "I" statements for feelings.
4. If you fall into blame, apologise and come back to the table.
5. Invite the other person's needs *on this subject* onto the table.
6. Take time to reach YES! solutions rather than pleasing each other.

Example of "Needs on the Table" communication
Thanks for agreeing to test something a bit different. I like the idea of having a structure to share what's disturbing me. My challenge is that when I'm upset and you interrupt me with a suggested solution, I conclude that you don't care about my feelings. I need to express myself fully without being interrupted, before I'm ready for a solution, and just feeling heard can be what I need. Can you tell me what is happening in you when you stop my expression of feelings, so I can see what you might need?

NEEDS THAT ARE HEARD HAVE A CHANCE OF BEING MET.

Story Time

Salt in the Wounds

You know those family stories that often get trotted out with memories of our childhood? There is one in my family called, "Virginia and the salt"; a memorable story for me because it repeatedly marred my mealtimes.

We always sat together for Sunday lunch in those days, five (and later six) of us around the table. I liked salt, and recall being deeply upset because no one would pass it to me. My silent tears dripped into my food on numerous occasions due to this unmet need.

The thing is, speaking up was a great challenge for me then, and I somehow had it in my head that others must know I needed the salt. However, at no point did I ask for it with either words or gestures. Understandably, my "no one will pass me the salt" tears were incomprehensible.

This behaviour is a clear example of outside-in relating – expecting the external world to deliver my needs on a plate! I eventually learned how to speak for myself and to put my needs on the table clearly and all was well, but I sometimes wonder whether we all have similar places – blind spots where we are so clear that our needs are blatantly visible to others that it does not occur to us to ASK SIMPLY AND CLEARLY.

* The Practice *

Between You and Me

Look in your journal at the list you made last week in answer to, "I get upset (or…) when s/he… because I need…"
Reread the needs that you identified as being important.

Take time to focus on any other important needs that might have cropped up since then. To do this, become aware of any upsets or disturbing behaviour in yourself in relation to someone else and ask:
 • What is my unmet need behind this emotion/behaviour?
E.g. You might be really stressed and feeling unwell because you need alone time to grieve and integrate a loss of some kind.

Again, if a need can be met by you, commit to doing this. Then decide what unmet needs (from another) you are ready to address.

During "Between You and Me" Week
Ask for a specific focussed time with the one(s) who might be able to help fulfil your need(s), and if it feels appropriate, say that you would like to use a simple way of sharing that you have been reading about which places sensitive issues in the space between you. If you can't get this person to join you in the exercise, you can at least practise your side silently by imagining anything sensitive you need to say landing *between you* rather than *aimed at* the other.

If they do agree, read aloud and then follow the Needs on the Table Steps, making sure that you fully express your needs and hear theirs. If they are not clearly stating their needs, guess what they might be needing behind the behaviour exhibited, e.g. "Do you think you need to interrupt my emotions because you don't like seeing me upset or because you are not comfortable with being emotional yourself?" Be gentle; there is often a deeper need than the one being expressed, e.g. I need to be loved (and won't be if I show vulnerability).

Beware, you might get a surprise instead of your expected outcome!

Supportive Resource: *Nonviolent Communication*, Marshall Rosenberg.[52]

What Do I Want?

Creating constructive outcomes

> ## * Opportunity *
>
> To manifest more of what we want in life by
> understanding and utilising
> the creative force of words.

*We cannot focus upon the weaknesses of one another and evoke
strengths. You cannot focus upon the things that you think
they are doing wrong,
and evoke things that will make you feel better.
You've got to beat the drum that makes you
feel good when you beat it.
And when you do,
you'll be a strong signal of influence
that will help them to reconnect with who they are.*

~ ABRAHAM-HICKS
(Wisdom Teachers)

When we focus on what we *do* want rather than what we don't, we set in motion creating the outcome of our desires. The human brain struggles to process negatives and has a tendency to do the opposite. Enid Blyton's Brer Rabbit made sure he was thrown into the safety of his familiar briar patch by begging his predator, "Roast me! Hang me, Brer Fox, only please *don't* throw me into the briar patch."

Diets are easily sabotaged by thinking about not eating the forbidden foods – I won't eat chocolate, hot bread, coffee, etc., and smoking is more likely to be stopped by saying, "I choose to breathe fresh air" than, "I'm not going to have a cigarette". Likewise: don't fall; don't touch the fire; don't drive too fast; you'll drop that if you're not careful, etc. implant the image of exactly what you don't want to happen. The mind will then try to negate the forbidden action as requested, but once seen, the image is usually stronger than our skill to make it disappear. I wonder if the chocolate bar slogan, "It's Not for Girls!" stopped females buying it or increased sales to both sexes.

When we strongly imagine and CLEARLY STATE WHAT WE *DO* WANT TO HAPPEN, it is easy for our energy to flow towards that. If we say, "I choose to be in healthy relationships", we implant that image. And instead of, "Watch you don't fall!" how about, "Hold onto the side" or simply imagining them being safe? Be vigilant also about vague expressions such as "I wish" or "I hope".

Steps to Creating Constructive Outcomes
(To be used in the week's practice)
    1. Identify something on which you find yourself focussing "negatively", e.g. "I can't stand being drained by her moaning".
    2. Ask, "What do I choose to happen?" Imagine clearly and specifically, the best outcome – including how it will feel in your body. What signs will help you recognise it when it appears?
    3. Is your choice in the best interest of all concerned? If not, refine it.
    4. Are you sure you can be open to this when it arrives? If your image produces fear, improve it or choose to face the fear.
    5. Take any needed actions towards the outcome, and enjoy!

Evidence for the power of "positive" words

In Doreen and Grant Virtue's book, *Angel Words: Visual Evidence of How Words Can Be Angels in Your Life,* there are hundreds of computer graphs which show whether a word is high-energy or low-vibrational and indicate the potential impact of saying something positively. (You can look at graphs inside the book on Amazon.[53])

Doreen Virtue says in a Facebook blog:[54]

> The mere act of altering your vocabulary and using life-affirming words can quickly and dramatically change your life in magical ways!

When she was recording a podcast with her son, Grant, he noticed that when she said the word "angel" the computer graph made the shape of angel wings. When they looked closer, they could see that each word had a unique pattern and so they began examining the shapes words made when spoken. They discovered that words that are generally considered positive produced a significantly larger pattern on the graph than those most people would describe as negative.

Doreen speaks in the book of their discovery:

> We were astounded by this visual representation of positive and negative utterances! Here was tangible evidence of high and low vibrations within speech. The positive words exhibited a much bigger impact, like light shining radiantly. Meanwhile, the negative ones looked tight and constricted.

In *Angel Words,* the graph of "I am open to criticism" is shown as small and "I am open to positive feedback" as large. "I have disabilities" is small, "I have abilities" large. "Broken" is small, "Whole" is large. The phrases "You shouldn't say negative words" and "Saying positive words can help you feel happy" have a similar meaning but the former graph is almost flat while the latter is large.

Will we enlarge our graphs and improve our life experience?

＊ The Practice ＊

What *Do* I Want?

Reread "Steps to Creating Constructive Outcomes" and quietly let your intuition tell you what the best situation would be to work on. One by one, copy and work with each step in your journal. Take your time to sense thoroughly into what achieving your desired outcome would feel, sound and look like. There may or may not be actions needed during the week. Sometimes the act of visualising is enough.

Remember, the word "want" itself can be limiting if said when feeling contracted or deprived – we can go on wanting something forever! When you use it, make sure it has a clear intention and commitment behind it, or use "I choose" or "I claim" instead.

During "What *Do* I Want" Week

In your daily interactions and inner-talk, be alert to your use of:

don't; not; won't; never; unconstructive statements/predictions; vague wishes or hopes.

Change your focus to what you *do* want to happen.

Particularly notice language that the body could take literally such as:

I can't move forward; he'll be the death of me; what a pain in the neck! I'm sick to the teeth of…

Say or think "cancel" or "change" when you catch anything that could be said more constructively or angled towards what you want (see examples).

Cancel ➜	Change to
◆ Stop that!	Would you please…
◆ Don't forget…	Remember to…
◆ She's really ill…	I'll imagine her healthy again
◆ I'm afraid he'll mess it up	I'll let go and trust him or offer help
◆ I'm really hurt	I feel hurt *and I can be comforted*
◆ There's no way out of this	I open to guidance and resolution
◆ I'm dying for a cup of tea	I'd love a cup of tea

Supportive Resource: Neuro Linguistic Programming (NLP).[55]

The Heart of Anger

Understanding anger and its causes

---

* Opportunity *

To come to know our own anger patterns
and to learn the difference between
healthy and harmful expressions.

Speak when you are angry
[without heart]
and you will make
the best speech you will ever regret.

~ AMBROSE BIERCE
(Journalist and Writer)

PLEASE NOTE
If you have major anger challenges, it is suggested you work
with a recommended psychotherapist to explore
your particular needs more deeply.

Anger is a wide-ranging and fiery topic with an unsavoury reputation. It covers irritation to raging fury and is triggered mainly by perceived threat, injustice or disappointment. These next four inter-related sections can be used together if need be. They have been left until now because many of the causes of anger have been worked with indirectly in the previous sections, leaving less anger to address.

There is an important distinction to make between unhealthy and healthy anger because anger per se is not the problem.

IT'S HOW WE EXPRESS ANGER THAT MATTERS.

Unhealthy (ineffective) anger is heartless: we are out of control, cut off from any care about the other's experience. It can be harmful because the anger's force is directed *at* others with blame and often intent to shame. In its extreme, it can turn to aggression and violence.

Healthy (hearty) anger allows us to express our boundaries, needs and deep feelings emphatically. It can succeed it getting others to listen if we have failed to be heard in other ways. Heartful anger needs us to keep part of ourselves in touch with our heart – our care for all concerned, and to listen deeply with "Zone ears" rather than "Wound ears" to the response (Weeks 11 and 12). It brings relief.

Prime Causes of Anger
- The ego perceives a threat and wants to be right/in control.
- Holding strong beliefs/assumptions/opinions/fears.
- Failing to get what we think we want or need.
- Suppressed emotion (by not directly facing the cause).
- Wanting, unconsciously, to cover other emotions – fear, grief, etc.
- Believing we are being victimised by something outside of us.
- Being triggered into past memories – maybe projecting on others.
- Low self-esteem – feeling diminished, at fault, helpless.
- Resistance: This shouldn't be happening!
- Intolerance of difference/diversity, i.e. The Judge.
- Chronic stress, lack of sleep, illness, medication side effects.

**Self-righteous justification of our anger will ensure its continuation.
Does the trigger really justify it?**

Anger Dynamics

By Carmella and M'haletta B'Hahn

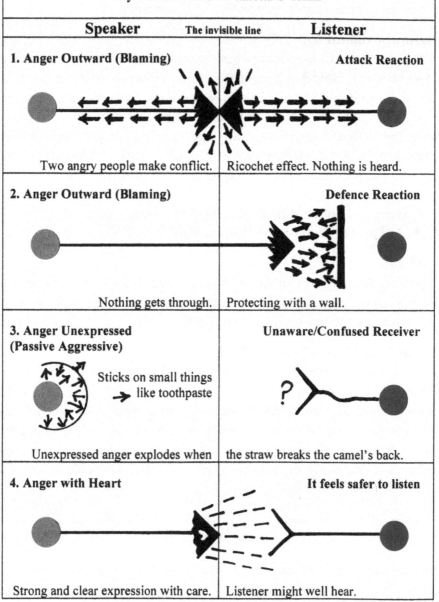

Speaker	The invisible line	Listener
1. Anger Outward (Blaming)		**Attack Reaction**
Two angry people make conflict.		Ricochet effect. Nothing is heard.
2. Anger Outward (Blaming)		**Defence Reaction**
Nothing gets through.		Protecting with a wall.
3. Anger Unexpressed (Passive Aggressive) — Sticks on small things like toothpaste		**Unaware/Confused Receiver**
Unexpressed anger explodes when		the straw breaks the camel's back.
4. Anger with Heart		**It feels safer to listen**
Strong and clear expression with care.		Listener might well hear.

* The Practice *

The Heart of Anger

This week is about becoming more conscious of anger dynamics and deciding how to bring more heart to our anger if this is missing.

Healthy or Unhealthy?

Look at the earlier descriptions of healthy and unhealthy anger, as well as the Anger Dynamics model and ponder on your conflict style. If you experience little or no conflict, you could be suppressing anger and turning it on yourself – a kind of implosion (See 3. on model). Anger that is unexpressed directly can be indirectly articulated in passive aggression such as: sullenness; sarcasm; refusal to help, or it can leak out through minor irritations, like getting overly upset by the toothpaste tube being squeezed incorrectly. Make notes and answer:

- ◆ What do I normally do with feelings of irritation or anger?
- ◆ Do I usually express anger with or without care of the other?

The Causes

Copy the "Prime Causes of Anger" list into your journal; reread it and star the most common causes of your annoyance or anger. Write freely about any new awareness and extend the list if need be.

During "The Heart of Anger" Week

In order to begin building a connection (neural pathway) between anger and your heart, carry any tangible heart-shaped object/cut out card in your pocket all week. Every time you notice irritation or anger in yourself or another, touch the heart and bring heart into the situation in your way. A kind thought or silent blessing to yourself or them might be enough. Or, you could authentically express your truth with heart (Week 23) or address your/their needs (Weeks 36 and 37).

When your own irritation or anger has passed, check the list for what you think was the real cause behind the external trigger. Is it starred?

What had the most meaning for you this week that you will carry on?

Supportive Resource: *Emotional Intimacy,* Robert Augustus Masters.[56]

This is the three-quarter mark.

Well done for having come this far!
Keep on keeping on.

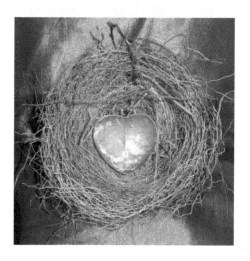

Reminding you to:
Return to your heart repeatedly –
to the core of awareness from which any words
will radiate with a resonance that
has more chance of being heard.

*The biosphere is not a collection
of inert and determinate objects,
but an ongoing communion
of living subjects.*

~ THOMAS BERRY
(Priest and Eco-theologian)

WEEK 40

Fire Prevention

Minimising conflict

> ## * Opportunity *
>
> To recognise and catch the first flame of
> anger before it burns anyone.

Anger is a signal,
and one worth listening to.

~ HARRIET LERNER
(Clinical Psychologist)

P revention is better than cure, they say. So, the ideal approach is perhaps to continue working on a healthy overall way of relating, as well as having strategies to employ, the moment anger-triggers arise. A list of strategies follows, most of which we have already visited and practised in other weeks.

Remember: ANGER ARISES FROM A COMBINATION
OF WHAT'S HAPPENING EXTERNALLY AND
OUR INTERNAL THOUGHTS AND BELIEFS ABOUT IT.

Ways of Preventing/Minimising *Our Own* Anger

• Recognise our first bodily signs of anger and learn to STOP and CHOOSE direction when triggered.

                       Fight
                         ↗
Trigger → STOP & → Calming → Speak with heart → Find solutions
        CHOOSE strategies
                         ↘
                       Flight

• Agree to talk about and clear upsets before they grow bigger.
• Avoid using inflammatory language and exaggeration (see over).
• Intuit our unmet needs behind our anger and address them.
• Use "I statements" to authentically share experience.
• Release blame ("you" statements) and right/wrong thinking.
• Listen with "Zone Ears" rather than "Wound Ears"(Week 12).
• Practise self-compassion. Emotional pain hides behind anger.
• Stay in the present with our feelings and what we know is true.
• Take responsibility for being the cause of our emotion.
• Take care of our sleep, diet, stress levels etc.
• Remember: Our differences help clarify what *we* think/want.

Ways of Preventing/Minimising *Others'* Anger

• Breathe and relax
• Give them full attention
• Listen deeply and reflect back – especially feelings
• Suggest calming strategies
• Offer help towards solution

Story Time

Preventing Escalation

A story sticks in my mind on this topic that I read in Daniel Goleman's book, *Social Intelligence*. It recounts a situation that confronted a group of American soldiers during the second US invasion of Iraq.

The platoon was on a mission to find someone at a local Mosque who might assist in distributing relief supplies. A mob began to gather when they approached the mosque, obviously afraid that the soldiers presented a threat to their holy shrine – or maybe coming to arrest their spiritual leader. The soldiers, who were heavily armed, as usual, were soon surrounded by hundreds of devout Muslims, shouting and gesticulating as they moved in closer.

> The commanding officer, Lieutenant Colonel Christopher Hughes, thought fast.
> Picking up a loudspeaker, he told the soldiers to "take a knee", meaning to kneel on one knee.
> Next he ordered them to point their rifles toward the ground.
> Then his order was, "smile".
> At that the crowd's mood morphed. A few people were still yelling, but most were now smiling in return. A few patted the soldiers on the back, as Hughes ordered them to walk slowly away backward – still smiling.

Excerpt from *Social Intelligence*, Daniel Goleman.[57]

This commanding officer stayed calm enough to retain a clear head to think fast in a small window of time. This window was his choice point, where, in this case, lives could have been lost or saved. Strong reactive emotion floods and clouds the thinking brain making clear decisions difficult, if not impossible.

* The Practice *

Fire Prevention

To get the most out of this full section, follow *all* the suggestions.

1. Allow a memory to arise of a time you became angry. What was the trigger and what happened in your body? E.g. "She assumed that my intention was the opposite of what it was. I became breathless, felt an urge to defend myself, and my lips went tight." Write these reactions down and be on the lookout for any similar bodily cues this week. They signal your "choice point" – the moment conflict could be prevented from escalating (including unexpressed inner conflict).

2. Decide to test out talking about any small upsets *before* they escalate, and consider making a pact with someone to do this in your relationship.

3. Circle on the "Preventing/Minimising Anger" lists any other strategies that you think could particularly help you.

During "Fire Prevention" Week
Do your best to employ all three of the things above: 1. Notice your body's reactions that signal a choice point, and de-escalate any anger. 2. Share small upsets. 3. Use any strategies you circled.

Watch out for inflammatory, emotive language and exaggeration. Look at the following words and imagine how you feel when someone uses them in relation to your behaviour.
> I feel… rejected, abused, ignored, misunderstood, used, cheated, manipulated, betrayed, forgotten, invaded, disrespected.

These are *not* feelings or facts; they are conclusions about the behaviour of others that can easily sound accusatory – the subtext is "you did this to me". Also, most people exaggerate when emotional. Notice whether you are being truthful when emotionally charged.

What learning from this week will you employ in the future?

Supportive Resources: *Conscious Communication*, Miles Sherts.[58]
Men Are From Mars, Women Are From Venus, John Gray.[59]

WEEK 41

Standing My Ground

Remaining centred when facing anger

* Opportunity *

To discover ways of responding to anger and
strong emotion in others that leave us feeling
more grounded and empowered.

*If you say one thing
that I have the urge to defend,
that thing is the very pearl inside me
waiting to be discovered.*

~ BYRON KATIE
(Author and Self-awareness Facilitator)

There is a big difference between *standing* our ground and *defending* our ground, when confronted with anger or strong emotion. "Standing my ground" is what I am calling the centred way. Attack and defence are opposite sides of the pendulum swing – neither comes from centre. And the urge to defend begs the question: What part of me truly needs defending? Ego perhaps? If I think my beliefs and opinions are *who I am*, I will defend them rigorously (Look Who's Talking – Week 3).

Have you ever done this exercise? You ask someone to push you in the chest and find yourself falling backwards and off balance; next you relax, feeling your core extending right into the ground, and when pushed a second time, find that you are immoveable. Simply by intention and focus you feel grounded and empowered.

When we find this empowered place, we immediately dispel the common premise: I can be offended, pushed over, diminished by others and need to defend my integrity. From centre we know that:

> ANOTHER'S ANGER BELONGS ENTIRELY TO THEM,
> NO MATTER WHAT WE HAVE DONE.

This balanced position of strength allows clear guidance about how to be and what to do in relation to another's confronting behaviour, and that guidance is unlikely to include attack or defence.

Ways to Stand Our Ground
- Respectfully and calmly leaving until the anger has diminished.
- Staying put, affirming our own safety and feeling the discomfort.
- Keeping in touch with who *we* are and holding an image of who *they* are beyond their temporary anger and limitations.
- Releasing any vestige of thought of the other as our opponent.
- Asking for more, e.g. "Please help me understand more about this", and listening for the pain behind the anger.
- Admitting our own contribution to the conflict and holding them accountable for theirs. (Avoid taking responsibility for what's theirs).
- Stating our own needs and boundaries, e.g. I need less volume to hear better and I want you to aim your anger *between us* not *at* me.
- Agreeing to disagree. (Is there a need to stand in the same place?)

Story Time

Saved by Assertion

I was nineteen and having an adventurous spell of volunteering in a kibbutz community in Israel. On a free weekend, I went alone to Jerusalem and, after a day of exploring the city, I set off on what I thought was the worn old tourist path up the Mount of Olives to see the spectacular view of the walled city from the summit.

It turned out that this was not the safe main route with its constant stream of pilgrims. It was a parallel, look-alike track and I was alone in my meandering. As I walked, with the sun burning down on me, I saw something strange in my peripheral vision. Several male workers on the neighbouring hillsides seemed to be making hand signals to each other. Then they started moving – about five of them – towards me. They were closing in fast and soon would be surrounding me. My legs went to jelly and my heart thudded. I tasted fear in my mouth. Something was about to be taken from me – my money, my passport, my body? What would it be? They were all half dressed, smeared with dirt and leering, so I imagined my body was at the forefront of their agenda.

As they stood there, a few feet away now on all sides, I silently shouted for help to any benevolent force listening. To this day, I can hardly believe the response. It was as if an assertive force of massive proportions came through me and into the earth. In that moment I knew, without thinking, that my strength of connection with myself needed to be greater than their collective intention. A surge of anger, that in words would have translated as, "I WILL *NOT* BE VIOLATED", went through my body, and I swear my hands shot, of their own volition, into a poised karate pose I'd never learned. I felt invincible as I spat out the question, "You know karate?" implying by my tone that I was proficient.

The tables turned fast as they nervously looked at each other – indecision and shock registering. This was not the victim they had expected. What to do? One of them twizzled on his heel and scampered away and, like sheep, the others swiftly followed.

The view from the top of the hill was particularly spectacular!

* The Practice *

Standing My Ground

Standing our ground means being assertive, and the story suggests that when we open ourselves to a force greater than our limited ego, perhaps we will simply know how to assert ourselves. Assertion is an effective alternative to fight, flight, or freeze reactions and can include choosing to surrender totally as the best option.

Assertiveness Exercise

The purpose of this exercise is to learn to realize quickly when we are being aggressive or submissive so that we are in a position of choice in the future to be assertive. I dare you to throw feeling silly to the wind and *do* it, either alone or in your partnership or group.

- Remember a time when you felt aggressive and without care of others. Freely move and fully express this aggression bodily. Freeze and notice your body posture, feelings and what stands out most.

- Now remember a situation in which you felt submissive and compliant – as if you didn't matter much – and express this as fully as possible. Stop and notice your stance, feelings, etc. as before.

- Lastly, remember a time you felt assertive – strong, kind and confident with a right to be fully seen and heard. Express this actively and then notice as many details as you can about how that feels.

Write about these stances and feelings of aggression, submission and assertion. Hopefully, you will now recognise future choice points and can consciously choose to bring in the body stance of assertion.

During "Standing My Ground" Week

Reread the exercise of being pushed over and find someone with whom to experience this, even if you have done it before. Practise using this immoveable earth connection at any time you need it. Also, reread "Ways to Stand Our Ground", mark those that sound most useful and watch out for ways of using them.

Note what has made an impression on you re. this week's topic.

Resolution and Retrieval

Clearing and salvaging relationships

---

* Opportunity *

To resolve painful dynamics and retrieve
relationships that can be saved.

---

*Are you open
to the soft moment
in the middle of everything harsh
that will reveal us to each other?*[260]

~ MARK NEPO
(Author and Poet)

PLEASE NOTE

*During this practice week, you may not need to use the steps
suggested. I have included them as a valuable resource for
whenever conflict does arise… as no doubt it will.*

I ndira Gandhi said, *You cannot shake hands with a clenched fist,* and so it is with resolution of conflict and retrieval of relationships.

CLARITY OF MIND IS WARPED BY STRONG EMOTION but when enough time has passed for the clenched fists to relax and both parties are ready to open towards each other and answer "yes" to this week's quote by Mark Nepo, then there is a chance for healing.

Five Steps to Conflict Resolution and Retrieval

1. Normalise the conflict[61]

Most conflict is normal; it is a call for change and a desire for things to be different. The need to resolve something offers the opportunity to build trust, understanding and a more resilient relationship.

2. Agree to meet

Set a time to meet, giving space first to calm down and do the inner work. Verbalise the intention to listen deeply and to find resolution.

3. Keep the disagreement to yourself

Avoid rallying support for your rightness. Talk in confidence with someone you trust if you need help to understand your behaviour.

4. Do your inner work

Am I projecting on this person? Do they remind me of challenges with someone else, which are fuelling my feelings? What am I doing to contribute to this conflict? Where is my ego in this? Am I trying to prove I'm right? Do I feel better than or less than this person?

5. Meet and include the following:

- Take it in turns to share: "What happened for me is..." and listen deeply, without interrupting. Reflect back what you have heard and use The Curiosity Step (Week 26) to help understand.
- Avoid conjecture and use "I" statements for feelings.
- Bring your heart, head and vulnerability to the table.
- Stay authentic, present, and avoid exaggeration/catastrophising.
- Share how you contributed to the conflict and apologise.
- Take time to find win/win solutions rather than pleasing each other. Say what *you* are willing to offer to help heal the situation.
- Agree to disagree if necessary and share anything for which you are left feeling grateful.

* The Magic of Apology *

An apology is the superglue of life.
It can repair just about anything.

~ LYNN JOHNSTON
(Cartoonist)

♦ Be sincere; apologise only when you truly mean it.

♦ Honestly acknowledge any "offence" and accept responsibility.

♦ Explain but *don't* excuse.

♦ Ask: What can I do to help heal this?

♦ Don't expect forgiveness, but if given, gratefully accept.

> *Example:*
> *I am so sorry for being this late. I expect you've been as*
> *worried and upset as I have. I was stuck behind an accident*
> *and had forgotten to charge my phone. Can I take you out*
> *to eat if the dinner is ruined?*

Apology can transform
the clumsiest moment into a gracious gift.

~ MARGARET LEE RUNBECK
(Author)

* The Practice *

Resolution and Retrieval

This chapter, as with the previous three, is a particularly useful resource when conflict arises, but in the meantime it will surely help to be prepared. You may not have anything obvious to resolve or retrieve but perhaps there is someone who needs to know that you still care about and value them after a past tricky exchange.

Sit quietly and tune in to anything that has happened in any of your relationships that could benefit from a clearing of some description – either a formal meeting, if serious, or an informal exchange.

Ask yourself:
+ What specific actions do I commit to taking towards resolving any misunderstandings and retrieving a relationship?

Actions could involve an apology (see The Magic of Apology), a clearing chat over tea, or a full Resolution and Retrieval meeting applying the five steps laid out earlier.

During "Resolution and Retrieval" Week

Set about initiating any intended actions you have written about and apologise in any situation you think it could help. Seemingly irreparable damage can be mended by an apology when it is done with sincere regret.

Beware "I'm sorry *you* feel that way", which just won't work. We don't have to take responsibility for having catalysed another's discomfort if this doesn't ring true but we can acknowledge hurt feelings and express concern without making ourselves wrong: "I am aware that our conversation has left you feeling upset. Is there anything I can do that would help right now?"

What worked well for you this week?

Note: If you don't feel safe to meet alone, contemplate using a mediator – someone to witness and keep you on track with the steps listed.

Supportive Resources: *Difficult Conversations*, Stone, Patton and Heen.[62]
The Courage To Love, Malcolm Stern and Sujata Bristow.[63]

The Embrace

Welcoming all and sundry

> ### * Opportunity *
>
> To relax more and more as we drop the stress
> of resistance and make friends with
> the reality before us.

The shift now is from
heroic conquest
to reverent embrace.

~ ROGER BROOKE
(Jungian Psychologist)

Ancient wisdom tells us to yield rather than to set ourselves in opposition to anything that seems to oppose us. The Persian poet, Rumi, implores us to embrace our difficulties because, *the wound is the place where the light enters you.* But the off-balanced ego disagrees and sabotages fruitful outcomes by resisting what it doesn't like or want to experience. It swells with the idea of controlling and changing things to get its personal agenda met. And a fruitful outcome for all is highly unlikely when relating from this position.

Embracing, accepting and welcoming the reality of what is in front of our noses, is perhaps a panacea for peace. Many of us believe this to be so: we have heard about the wisdom of yielding; we know that resisting inevitable change causes stress; we might say we are being educated by the university of life, and yet still we instinctively resist anything that feels unpleasant, rather than opening to its gifts.

When I started writing this chapter, I had an onslaught of cramp in my foot. I was wiggling and stretching it, jumping up and down – anything to avoid the discomfort. Then, because of the "embracing" focus, I tested welcoming the cramp and allowing it to express its crampyness. I simply stopped resisting and relaxed as best I could. It twisted strenuously initially but then, the more I surrendered, the more it lessened its grip. All I had done was shift from fighting to embracing it, and as I relaxed, I remembered Byron Katie – self-confessed "lover of what is" – saying,

IF YOU ARGUE WITH REALITY, YOU WILL LOSE.

If we truly want to let go of our resistant position, it is possible, with practise, to switch our perception in an instant and melt away stress and irritation. The most testing of life's challenges can be embraced. Byron Katie aspires to live by her belief:

When you know that whatever you need is what you get, life becomes paradise.

This could be too big a leap of belief for some, so here's another Rumi quote from a different angle that could support our move to embrace what is rubbing us up the wrong way:

If you are irritated by every rub, how will your mirror be polished?

The Guest House

This being human
is a guest house.
Every morning a new arrival.

A joy, a depression, a meanness,
some momentary awareness comes
as an unexpected visitor.

Welcome and entertain them all
even if they are a crowd of sorrows
who violently sweep your house
empty of its furniture.

Still treat each guest honourably,
they may be clearing you out
for some new delight.

The dark thought, the shame,
the malice, the fear,
meet them at the door laughing
and invite them in.

Be grateful for whoever comes,
for each has been sent
as a guide from beyond.

~ RUMI
Translation by Coleman Barks

* The Practice *

The Embrace

So, how exactly do we make this embrace – this shift in perception that dissolves stress? Reframing is a simple, effective tool.

Reframing: The transformation of meaning.[64]
The way we "frame" anything creates a meaning, which evokes a response. Constructive reframing creates a new perspective that evokes a beneficial response. Conversely, "spin", used extensively by media, advertisers and politicians, seeks to meet its own agenda.

Make a note of a situation you are resisting and/or upset about and ask yourself whether you are ready to reframe it? If not, perhaps ask "why not?" before choosing a situation you can say yes to. Use the following questions and examples to help you to reframe it in various ways. Note changes in your feelings and responses to the situation.

Questions to help reframe and gain benefit from difficulties
- What else could this mean?   • What can I learn from this?
- What was the positive intention of this behaviour?
- What quality does this situation call from me?
- Where and when could this behaviour be useful?

Reframing Examples
- I feel hurt when they repeatedly point out what doesn't work.
They care enough to want to make things better.

- This is frightening. *I will find out about my level of courage.*

- A friend e-mails you an invite to his cabaret birthday party, which clashes with the date of another cabaret to which you are committed. The RSVP e-mail subject line could be reframed from "Disappointing Clash" to *"Synchronised Cabarets!"*

During "The Embrace" Week
Your task this week is to practise reframing at every opportunity and see how much can be harvested from challenges. Discuss your successes and note what worked best for you that you will repeat if possible.

WEEK 44

Advanced Forgiveness

Dissolving grievances

> ### * Opportunity *
>
> To clear the harmful effects that
> holding grudges brings.

When you hold a grudge,
you want someone else's sorrow
to reflect your level of hurt
but the two rarely meet.

~ STEVE MARABOLI
(Author and Motivational Speaker)

There is an advanced kind of forgiveness that occurs naturally by itself when we can say and truly mean,

THANK YOU *FOR GIVING* ME
THE GIFT OF THIS DIFFICULTY.

Grievances dissolve with gratitude because it no longer feels as if there is something to forgive. For this dissolving to occur, we will have managed to embrace who or whatever catalyzed our grievance – as described in last week's lesson. This level of forgiveness is impossible if we believe ourselves to be at the mercy of outside circumstances. In extreme situations it can be a very tall order.[65]

Sometimes we want to hold onto the familiar discomfort of grievances, and the complaints and sense of righteousness that accompanies them, and sometimes we would let them go if we knew how. If we don't release them, our energy will continue to leak out in trails that bind us to anyone or thing we believe has "wronged" us and will perpetually trigger resentment when anything similar occurs.

Deepest forgiveness requires:
- Allowing and appropriately expressing any feelings that arise.
- Stepping out of the right/wrong mindset (Week 14).
- Recognizing that the "perpetrator's" behaviour is reflecting *their* conditioning, and practising empathy (Week 26).
- Remembering that our true self cannot be harmed (Week 3).
- Ignoring the ego's pull to take things personally (Week 7).
- Looking for the gift that dovetails with something we need to learn and feeling grateful when it is found.
- Holding the "perpetrator", including self, accountable and suggesting amends (not always possible).

Creating a symbolic ritual can be helpful for some, such as lighting a candle and speaking to a photo of someone before burning something that represents the grievance between you, or planting something beautiful to represent a new beginning. Also, accepting a sincere apology, if offered, from another or self, will speed full forgiveness.

Story Time

Wisdom in Forgiving

Mohandas K. Gandhi's grandson, Arun Gandhi, is dedicated to helping youth to deal with conflict non-violently. In 2001, I was privileged to interview him in Memphis, Tennessee, USA for my book *Mourning Has Broken.*[66] Around the walls hung a series of enormous photographs of his famous grandfather, which cast a peaceful presence about the room.

Arun lived in South Africa as a child where he suffered terribly from the prejudice of apartheid: *I was beaten by white South Africans for being too black and by black South Africans for being too white, and it affected me very deeply.* His parents had devoted their lives to non-violent and political change in South Africa – a movement started by his grandfather in 1893. In his early teens, during a tumultuous period in India's history, Arun went to live with and be tutored by his grandfather in India. *His love was overpowering and he lived out in front of me the values he wanted me to learn. "Be the change you wish to see," he used to say.*

Then, on Friday January 30, 1948 came the day that would be etched in Arun's mind forever. He returned home from school to find his mother on the phone, sobbing. *She put the phone down and told me that grandfather had been assassinated. He had been shot at point blank range and fell to the ground with his hands together in prayer saying, "Ram, Ram"* [a Hindu deity]. *I was absolutely stunned. I could see the time I had spent with him flash across my mind – the love he showered on me, the lessons he taught me. My immediate reaction, after I got over the shock, was one of tremendous anger. I wanted to throttle the person who committed this heinous crime. That's when my parents reminded me of the lesson I was taught by grandfather about using anger positively. They told me that grandfather would have wanted me to forgive his assassin.*

The assassin was hanged, against the family's wishes. Much later, Arun and Sunanda, his wife, visited his accomplice who was serving a life sentence in prison. *Although I found him ignorant and unrepentant, I saw the wisdom in forgiving. I could have carried hate in my heart forever and ruined my life, but instead we left him to deal with his life and conscience. One could so easily scream and be violent and make enemies of people who have perpetrated that kind of crime, but the positive use of the anger is to turn things around and see that you can make some change.*

Arun used the energy of his anger to create peace projects including *The Gandhi Institute for Nonviolence* – the location of our interview.

* The Practice *

Advanced Forgiveness

Sit and contemplate these two questions:
  - ◆ Do I hold a grudge that I am ready to release, against anyone?
  - ◆ What do I want or need to forgive myself for?

Of course the answers could be "no one" and "nothing". If you are absolutely sure about that, congratulations! Take the week off and watch out for this forgiveness theme raising its head in the future.

Choose just one to thing to focus on now and then decide how and when to deal with any others. Firstly, with the grudge or "transgression" in mind, slowly reread the "Deepest Forgiveness Requires" list and check out where you stand with each of these steps, circling those to which you want to give some attention. Go back to the chapters cited if you want to go deeper. Some steps can be done internally right now; others will need action.

When you have finished what you can of the above, devise a plan of your own creation as a final completion to your forgiveness process or use either of the following suggestions if they appeal.

Write a letter of forgiveness to yourself or your "transgressor" and post it… or not. (Do this only after completing your inner work.)

Create a release ritual as suggested previously. Use your imagination – plan to burn, bury, put in a stream, untie/cut something symbolic. Invite witnesses if you think it will be supportive.

During "Advanced Forgiveness" Week
Carry out the plan you have made and write about the results. Do you now feel clear or is there still some residue of grudge or self-blame that needs further addressing? You will know you have succeeded by the degree of softness you feel towards the other or yourself.

What are the next steps, if any?

Supportive Resource: *Radical Forgiveness*, Colin C. Tipping.[67]

It's a Mystery

Living in the unknown

> ## * Opportunity *
>
> To discover the relaxation and relief
> that comes with
> not having to know the answers.

*All the great pioneers
walked in unknown territories.*

~ THOMAS HUEBL
(Contemporary Spiritual Teacher)

L ike the dark to an imaginative child, the unknown can be a scary place. Sometimes it takes courage to enter simple unknowns such as going though the door to a party alone, starting a new job, talking to people who seem different, or buying things online. We generally like to be prepared, to know, be in control, have the right answers and second-guess outcomes. The ego seems terrified of ignorance and seeks safety in knowledge. But knowledge alone, as useful and impressive as it may be, will not make us wise or completely safe.

Lao Tzu, founder of Taoism and author of the *I Ching*, said,
> IN PURSUIT OF KNOWLEDGE, SOMETHING IS ACQUIRED.
> IN PURSUIT OF WISDOM SOMETHING IS DROPPED.

It is this "dropping" into the unknown, the mystery (already visited in Bows and Arrows – Week 31) that this section is all about.

The intellect (the cognition and rational mental processes gained through external input rather than internal[68]) loves wrestling with problems and actively seeking answers, whereas, "in-tuition" arises from the inside out and seems to love responding to spacious enquiry. Wisdom often shows itself in the humble void of unknowing, where questions patiently await a response, trusting in perfect timing.

Sitting in the unknown allows our senses to become more sharply alert to "in-tuition". We are then free to respond to the unfolding dynamic of the moment. Surprises often arise from this space.

Highly effective leaders and group facilitators will have a general plan, a direction in which they want to go to complete the task, *and* they are able to put down their notes and agenda and trust in their ability to respond to the live dynamics and needs of the group. The same is true of great counsellors and therapists: each session is a venture into unknown territory with trust that a suitable route will present itself without needing to be mapped out in advance.

We can't fly if we are holding on to the edge – to the known, to the comfortable, to our notes. Sometimes we need to just trust, risk and let the wind take us to places that we couldn't otherwise reach.

Come Play with Trust

Trust is calling you out to play,
to surrender your known life ~ just for a day.

The invitation says, *"Come rest a while*
in innocence, sweet as a toddler's smile.
Sense the relief of not having to achieve;
nothing to work out, to know or believe.
Surrender and open to this childlike space;
let go into this knowledge-free state of grace."

You're invited to visit the infinite unknown;
where, no doubt, seeds of wisdom are sown.
If you accept, if you take heart, and leap...
the magic of mystery will be yours to keep.

Trust is calling you out to play.

Will you skip out of our mind ~
               at least for a day?

~ CARMELLA B'HAHN

**How does learning to live comfortably with mystery
affect our relationships?**
It creates a much more relaxed field in which to
communicate, devoid of the
"dog with a bone" energy that has to know the answer.

* The Practice *

It's a Mystery

Sometimes a courageous leap into the unknown is called for without clear direction or guarantee of results. At other times the wisest response to not knowing is to hold a space of enquiry until what we need to know becomes clear. Ask yourself these questions:
- How comfortable do I feel when I don't have the answers?
- Is there anything in my life right now that would benefit from:

a) Me taking a leap or step into the unknown?

b) Me holding a space of enquiry around it?

Holding an enquiry about something is an invaluable tool. It needs us to hone the most useful question/s and to *await* clarity. It is the question that draws the answer. Craft an enquiry question now, e.g.
- What is it that stops my communication from flowing with …?
- What do I need to do/be to be fully receptive to clarity about …?

Tips

1. Let go and live with your question a while rather than thinking up answers. Allow space for insight to present itself in its own timing.

2. Be careful with "why" questions. These can easily feel blaming and elicit justification rather than insight, e.g. "Why don't I leap when I know I should?" (an admonishment) versus "Why is it that part of me still feels the need to hold on?" (caring interest).

3. When you focus on a problem and what is wrong, it can cause disempowerment and inertia, but when a constructive enquiry is made, such as, "What possibility does this situation hold for us?" it can feel as if a door has swung open.

During "It's a Mystery" Week

Practise relaxing into *not knowing*, at every opportunity. Allow questions you have formed to percolate, and watch for the different ways in which clarity appears. Perhaps you are ready to take a leap or step into the unknown? Note in your journal what worked well.

Supportive Resource: *The Art of Powerful Questions*, Eric E. Vogt, Juanita Brown and David Isaacs.[69]

Marvellous Mistakes

Releasing the concept of failure

> ## * Opportunity *
>
> To expand our wisdom, knowledge and
> strength by harvesting the insights
> from what we call "mistakes".

*There is no failure, only feedback.
Failure is an unprecedented opportunity
to learn something
you wouldn't otherwise notice.*

~ An N.L.P. Presupposition

Failure and mistakes do not exist in the same way when we are living the paradigm that embraces everything for our learning. When we reside in ego, however, failure is seen as unacceptable – a shameful blow to our rightness and how we want to be perceived by others. When we make what we *do* a strong part of our identity we will cringe at our "mistakes", blame others for theirs, deny, defend and even lie to protect our fictitious self-image… or beat ourselves up. And our Egometer will be swinging with its "better than" or "worse than" extremes (Ego Watch – Week 7).

Those of us who do not accept our own imperfections and who fear criticism (often borne of a critical or abusive parental figure) can feel an impulsive need to justify and explain our "imperfect" behaviour. This will block our learning because, as author Richard Bach said,

Argue for your limitations and sure enough they are yours.[70]
Revisiting Who Said That? – Week 20 could help here.

"Perfectionist" is a reputable label for one who strives for the perfect outcome, but when we judge anything less than perfect as a failure, our self-worth (and our opinion of others) diminishes accordingly. As a child, my son screwed up every drawing he made that didn't meet his ambitious standard, but had he applied his own excellent critical eye without seeing failure, he might have improved a lot faster.

Of course, we all do things that we would rather not have done due to the consequent effects – some more consequential than others – but there is a world of difference between, a) framing what we did as a failure and b) saying, "Ouch, that didn't work! What is the learning here and how can I help to heal or improve this?"

PEOPLE ARE MORE LIKELY TO REMEMBER THE REACTION TO A MISTAKE RATHER THAN THE MISTAKE ITSELF.

And who has not experienced a marvellous mistake such as taking a "wrong" turn and finding something extraordinary? Post-its wouldn't exist if the super-strong adhesive that 3M was developing hadn't "failed". But it needed an innovative attitude to notice the marvel in the "mistake" and to create a re-useable, low-tack adhesive instead.

If you're not prepared to be wrong,
you'll never come up with anything original.

~SIR KEN ROBINSON
(Advisor on Education in the Arts)

Mini Story

Thomas Edison tried two thousand different materials in search of a filament for the light bulb. When none worked satisfactorily, his assistant complained, "All our work is in vain. We have learned nothing."

Edison replied very confidently, "Oh, we have come a long way and we have learned a lot. We know that there are two thousand elements which we cannot use to make a good light bulb."

Anon

Yesterday's gone.
There's nothing you can do to bring it back.
You can't "should've" done something.
You can only DO something.
Renew yourself. Release that attachment.
Today is a new day!

~ ECKHART TOLLE
(Author and Consciousness Teacher)

* The Practice *

Marvellous Mistakes

Ponder on your relationship with "mistakes" and perfectionism. It could help if you focus on your reaction to a specific incident. Now apply the steps below to this or any other "mistake" and see how they could have helped at the time… or can still help now if you act.

How to make mistakes useful (if not marvellous)
- **Reframe** the notion of "mistakes" and "failure", e.g. failure is feedback – (See The Practice, The Embrace – Week 43).
- **Face and tell the truth** about your mistake with compassion for self. Others' initial reaction to our truth could be intense, but at least we will keep our integrity if we remain honest.
- **Acknowledge any inconvenience caused, accept responsibility and apologise** (see Apology – Week 42).
- **Focus on what can be done to improve the situation, and gratefully reap the learning.** When we focus on the constructive, we create an infectious, upward, feel-good spiral, just as we create an infectious, downward, feel-bad spiral by focussing on what we did "wrong" and our guilt.

During "Marvellous Mistakes" Week
1. Ask for a reality check from someone who knows you well:
- How do you perceive my behaviour in relation to my own and others' mistakes and failure?

Make notes of anything new and act to correct anything you choose.

2. Dare to reveal, to someone you trust, a part of yourself that you usually hide, and as you do so, be open to noticing the silver lining as well as the cloud. What have you hidden to avoid being cast in a bad light? E.g.:

Reveal a part of your body if you see it as a mistake of nature; share an aspect of yourself you are ashamed about; confess a guilty secret.

The purpose is to shed light on emotional burdens we carry by having framed things as mistakes or wrongdoings, and to ease some of these by being witnessed.

Write down what worked and what you will take forward.

Question the Label

Ceasing stereotyping

* Opportunity *

To feel more open-hearted towards people
of all kinds by noticing the gifts offered by
individuality and differences.

*We have created so many labels
we cannot see through them
to the soul of the human being.*

~ ARUN GANDHI
(Peace Worker)

There are numerous ways in which we put people and experiences into labelled boxes and thereby dismiss their individual essence. Stereotyping is a widespread way of "boxing". Thought-Bodies – Week 21, began to address this labelling activity.

Stereotyping means making generalisations about groups (often inaccurate and unflattering) that lead people to treat individuals in that group accordingly. It prejudges others and kindles expectations and assumptions. Stereotypes are possibly borne of some truth, but they take no account of individuality.

Common Stereotypes

Women are bad drivers; men love sport and don't feel deeply; the English are reserved; Italians are great lovers; Americans are brash; Jews are great at business; blonds are stupid; spiritual people are space cadets; lesbians look masculine; children hate good food; Pit Bulls are dangerous; politicians, bankers and journalists are corrupt.

In a swimming pool recently, when three teenage boys came in, a nearby swimmer turned to me and said, "I'm getting out of here, now!" She was gone before they touched the water. Because of her reaction, I thoroughly enjoyed the life force these youngsters were exuding in their play. She had stereotyped teenagers as "disruptive" and behaved accordingly. On a similar note, I overheard a man saying dismissively, "Bowden House is a commune of hippies". This conjured a radically different picture to the reality of my home and showed his ignorance. I was tempted to invite him to tea and an education about this unique community of impressive individuals.

STEREOTYPING AND GENERALISATIONS
CAN MISS THE RICHNESS OF OUR DIFFERENCES.

Labels, when used consciously, are sometimes helpful – a relief even. Generalisations can also be useful, however, if we want to make a general statement, it helps to *say so* because this shows that we don't actually mean "all", "everyone" or "everything" in the category about which we are speaking. We could say, "Speaking generally, I notice…" or "I am generalising widely here…"

Story Time

ADHD – Gift or Label?

This story, told by Sir Ken Robinson, international advisor on education in the arts, in his 2006 TED Talk: *How Schools Kill Creativity*, has been heard by millions, but I never tire of the power of its message, so will share it here as a perfect example of seeing through the label to the essence.[71]

There was a little girl called Gillian who couldn't concentrate or keep still in class and was causing disruption for both classmates and teachers. The school informed her parents that they suspected she had a learning disorder and suggested she might do better at a school for special needs. She would have probably been labelled ADHD today, but as Sir Ken said, "ADHD hadn't been invented yet!"

So mother and daughter went to see a psychologist and her mother spent a while describing her child's distracted behaviour while Gillian sat on her hands to stop herself fidgeting. She was very nervous although *she* didn't think she had a problem. The specialist listened and carefully observed Gillian before asking her mother to join him outside for a few moments. He asked Gillian to be patient a little longer and turned on the radio as they left.

The psychologist paused by a window into the room and said to her mother, "Just stand here for a moment, and watch what she does". Gillian was soon on her feet moving gracefully to the music and they observed her, transfixed. The psychologist finally turned to Gillian's mother and said, "You know, Mrs Lynne, Gillian isn't sick; she's a dancer. Take her to a dance school." She followed his advice and Gillian, thrilled to be with people like herself who "needed to move to think", flourished.

Gillian Lynne has had a dazzling career as a dancer and has choreographed some of the most successful musical theatre of all time, including *Cats* and *Phantom of the Opera*. Said Sir Ken, "Someone else might have put her on medication and told her to calm down… she just needed to be allowed to be herself."

✳ The Practice ✳

Question the Label

There is no journal work. Your task is to read the three examples below and get clear about what you will be looking out for this week. Stereotyping can be obvious and easy to catch and change if we choose to, or it can remain in our blind spot having been ingrained by our family or culture. Some stereotyping remains in our thoughts, unspoken but present in our attitude and affecting our behaviour.

1. Question statements that emerge from stereotypes
- Old folks shouldn't be allowed to drive.
Maybe this older person is going slowly for a good reason.
- My boy will stop hugging me when he's thirteen.
He might and he might not. Some teenagers hug their mothers.
- I'll probably be bored and boring when I retire.
Why? I could choose to make my life incredibly interesting.

2. Question generalisations
- Everyone/nobody/all…
Are there some people who are different?
- They never…
Was there a time when they did?
- Young/old people/men/women (any category) are…
What, all of them?

3. Question individual labels
- **Lazy:** could this mean *bored because she's not being stimulated?*
- **Slow learner:** could this mean *he learns in a different way?*
- **Disabled:** could this mean *her legs don't work but everything else does – including her brilliant brain?*

During the Week
Catch and question your use of stereotyping and labelling (spoken or unspoken) such as shown above, and fine-tune your language as far as you want to. Practise prefacing any generalisation you make with "Speaking generally…" or a phrase of your choice.

What had the most impact this week? Anything you are changing?

*Nothing outside yourself
can bring you home.*

~ JEFF FOSTER
(Author)

Recitation Practice

I have *a body, but I am* not *my body.*

I have *emotions, but I am* not *my emotions.*

I have *thoughts but I am* not *my thoughts.*

*I am what remains,
a pure centre of awareness,
an unmoved witness of all these
thoughts, emotions, feelings and desires.*

~ KEN WILBER

Roles in Persona

Examining the roles we play

> ## * Opportunity *
>
> To feel the freedom of stepping in and out of the
> roles we play, leaving us more connected with the
> "beingness" of who we are beyond them.

*The persona is that which
in reality one is not,
but which oneself
as well as others
think one is.*

~ CARL JUNG
(Psychiatrist and Psychotherapist)

There are countless roles to be played in the grand drama of life, which can become merged with who we think we are – our persona (see Jung's quote and Week 3's Identity Model). We can identify so closely with our roles, e.g. single mother, counsellor, jolly person, that we define ourselves by them and find comfort in the safety of their familiarity. Authentic, inside-out relating is impossible when we can't detach ourselves from the roles we play.

Our security lies in remembering that
WE CAN LOSE A ROLE BUT WE CAN'T LOSE WHO WE ARE.

Attachments to our work-life roles are often rudely revealed by unemployment or retirement, but why wait for external circumstance to offer the revelation of who we are? Roles are unavoidable and each one comes with criteria to be met and with status that influences the way we communicate. A role can range from being a vital and useful way of operating, to a mask we try to hide behind.

There are: relationship roles that we are born into and those we form through life; roles created by what we do in life; and others defined by character traits and learned behaviour. Here are some examples:

Relationships – all blood- and step- relationships, godparent, guardian, bachelor, partner, wife/husband, ex-partner, widow/er, neighbour, friend, colleague.

What we do – student, homemaker, labourer, artist, priest, actor, entrepreneur, teacher, doctor, psychotherapist, traveller, cleaner.

Character traits/behaviour – nurturer, joker/fun person, life and soul, rescuer/victim/persecutor,[72] devil's advocate, charmer, Eeyore (gloomy), solution-finder, mediator/peace-maker.

We can get caught in roles we habitually play but don't resonate with any more. Sometimes we are on automatic pilot, living unconsciously with a mismatch between our inside feelings and outside choices – a clash that does not support our health. It is up to us to align our inner selves with the roles we are playing now and to learn how to step in and out of them consciously. Roles that we use as masks are important to explore if we are choosing to live authentic lives.

Story Time

This story by Kahlil Gibran (Lebanese mystic and author of *The Prophet*) suggests that living without masks is a courageous act because to behave without the veil of illusion that they confer is to risk being seen as mad by our society.

How I Became A Madman
Kahlil Gibran (1918)

You ask me how I became a madman. It happened thus:

One day, long before many gods were born, I woke from a deep sleep and found all my masks were stolen – the seven masks I have fashioned and worn in seven lives. I ran maskless through the crowded streets shouting, "Thieves, thieves, the cursed thieves."

Men and women laughed at me and some ran to their houses in fear of me.

And when I reached the market place, a youth standing on a house-top cried, "He is a madman." I looked up to behold him; the sun kissed my own naked face for the first time. For the first time the sun kissed my own naked face and my soul was inflamed with love for the sun, and I wanted my masks no more. And as if in a trance I cried, "Blessed, blessed are the thieves who stole my masks."

Thus I became a madman…

An excerpt from *The Madman: His Parables and Poems*.[73]

* The Practice *

Roles in Persona

To recap: our persona is made up of roles that can help or hinder us according to our level of attachment to them, e.g. "Teacher" can be a useful role but we need to know how and when to drop it and to be willing to be a student as well. Roles used as masks can feel like protection, but ultimately prevent us from being ourselves.

In your journal, write **Roles I Play** in the middle of a page and using the previous examples of the three categories – Relationships, What we do, and Character traits/behaviour – brainstorm and fill the page with roles you play. If you are into drama, act some of them out.

Now take a little quiet time to ponder the following questions:
  ◆ Which of these roles, if any, do I define myself by?
  ◆ Which roles bolster or weaken my sense of self?
  ◆ Am I hiding anything behind any of these roles? What is that?

The power of choice becomes possible with awareness of the roles we play and we can then practise stepping in and out at will. When we step out of dovetailing roles, e.g. "mothering" and "mummy's boy", "critic" and "pleaser" or "victim" and "rescuer", others might not like it, but it will free them to release their roles also.

During "Roles in Persona" Week
Observe yourself and the roles you are playing at any given time. Notice how your behaviour and tone of voice differs in your various roles and how you change in relation to the roles that others play. How much is your behaviour based on what others expect of you rather than what you sense is the truly authentic you?

Eckhart Tolle expresses perhaps the ultimate aim in relation to roles:
> *...if you are present, you are not a father or mother, you are the alertness, the stillness, the Presence that is listening, looking, touching, even speaking. You are the being behind the doing.*[74]

Do you resonate with this aim of simply being your true self – your essence? If so, how are you doing?

WEEK 49

Actions Speak Louder

Hitting the spot with action

---

* Opportunity *

To increase feelings of safety and intimacy in our
relationships by validating our caring
words with supportive action.

To give pleasure to a single heart
by a single act
is better than a thousand heads
bowing in prayer.

~ MAHATMA GANDHI

Would you rather have someone tell you they care about you or show you with a loving act? Preferably both I imagine. Words can be powerful – especially if animated with feeling – but sometimes they won't hit the spot without the validation of action.

TANGIBLE SIGNS OF CARE ARE ABSORBED THROUGH MORE SENSES THAN WORDS AND HAVE LASTING IMPACT.

When I remember how others have expressed their care for me, I recall not words but actions: the flowers I've received; being driven four hours to an airport; offers of food when sick; children flinging their arms around my neck; gifts carefully thought about; poems composed for me; phone calls for no reason except to connect.

When relating to anyone remotely traumatised, it is especially important to use right brain functions – visuals, pictures, objects, actions or stories – because shock and strong emotion like grief and anger shut down the left brain, debilitating logic and verbal expression. Many of us will recognise a clouding of logic when angry or upset. Remember my story of the angry man's knife and my flower placed on the blade (Week 34)? That action spoke volumes. Likewise, being handed my boy's jacket to hug as a conduit for my grief after he had died was more effective than any words of counsel!

Of all the tributes in remembrance of those who died in the World Trade Center attacks in New York on September 11, 2001, one was called for year after year on the anniversary because it touched people so deeply. It is the *Tribute in Light* – two tower-like streams of coloured searchlights blasting light into the sky from the site.

Although varied, all the examples above represent the *out* bit of inside-out relating – they are external manifestations of feelings and thoughts, which give evidence of care. Without some form of tangible evidence, it can be difficult to know for sure that someone cares for us. Stepping out of our normal pattern to do something a bit different to show we care can bring enormous joy and reassurance – not to mention the joy that witnessing another's pleasure brings us.

Story Time

How We Know We Are Significant[75]
Dr Martin Brokenleg

This is a true story from Dr Martin Brokenleg, co-founder of *Circle of Courage*, whom I had the pleasure of meeting in the sacred Black Hills of Dakota, USA on several occasions. His parents were traditional Lakota people and his home at the time of the story was the Rosebud Reservation. He was then seventeen and studying away at school. Here are his words:

Christmas vacation came to an end. The winter weather was threatening, so my father decided it best that I fly back to school. A blizzard was coming in. My father left me at the downtown hotel in Rapid City, and he hurried back to the reservation. I got up early the next morning when it was still dark. The snow was blowing sideways, and I could not even see the ground. I called down to the front desk and found that the shuttle was going for the 6 am flight, which was still scheduled. I checked out of my room and sat down in the lobby near the window. Snow was blowing everywhere. An occasional car would go by, but there was almost no one outside.

The snow let up and I could see almost a half a block. A shadow passed under the streetlight, and someone was leaning into the wind heading toward the hotel.

The person was all wrapped up and came inside. She shook the snow off her Pendleton blanket, and I could identify that she was my father's cousin. She lived a couple of miles away. She had no car but had walked to see me before I departed. She came up to me and put her arms around me and said, "Son, I heard you were going back to school today and I wanted to come and see you. How is your mother and how is your father?" We sat down and talked until the shuttle bus pulled up. I stood up to go, and she stood up and put her arms around me. She said, "I want you to know that I am proud of you for staying in school. Someone in our family should have an education. You learn everything you can. I will think about you every day. I will pray for you every day." She wrapped the blanket around herself and walked back out into the blowing snow.

When someone cares for us amidst the blizzards of life, we know we are significant. This is not something that can be taught in words but can be communicated to others in how we treat them. Every teacher worth being a teacher knows that her students will forget what she says to them but they will never forget how she made them feel. That is the difference between learning something in the head and learning it in the heart.

* The Practice *

Actions Speak Louder

Sit quietly and let your mind visit some specific memories of when you felt moved by someone's expression of their care or love for you. This could be in relation to one person or several. Capture these memories in a nutshell in your journal and take a moment to focus on how you felt receiving these expressions of care.

Next, allow memories to arise of things that you have done for others that showed you care about them and get in touch with how you felt when planning these and watching them being received. Write these down too. Capture anything else that you feel is worth noting.

Now it's time for some fun. Identify one or two people who you think would benefit from knowing that you care about/love them. Hold them in your mind (one at a time if more than one) and imagine something that *they* might appreciate. Plan to do it this week if possible. Do your best to match their taste – for instance, some people are uncomfortable with surprises and some might not like anything expensive because of feeling obliged to reciprocate.

Here are some ideas to spark your own:
> Collect wild flowers and put them on the doorstep or table; slip a caring note into their pocket or bag; buy them a gift when it is not their birthday or traditional day for gift-giving; write "Thank you" in small stones in the garden; offer to babysit or give someone space to pamper themselves; make tea or clear up when you wouldn't normally; clean their shoes; read them their favourite poem/story; handwrite a letter or card and post it!

During "Actions Speak Louder" Week
Put your plan(s) into action and enjoy yourself. This is about creative positivity that could rekindle a relationship that needs a new spark. If you need reassurance that someone cares for you, you could ask, but perhaps begin by giving out the care you'd like to receive.

How did it turn out? Will you do something like this again?

In the Field

Building group resonance

> ### * Opportunity *
>
> To learn how to affect favourably the energy and
> outcome of a group experience or endeavour.

Set up a "field" into which people come.
If you can set a field that is open and loving,
with a clear intention and purpose,
you create a safe and supportive environment. When people walk
into that, it immediately influences them
and they come into synchronization
and resonance with the field.

~ ROBERT KENNY
(Professor and Author)

No man or woman is an island, as we saw in It's Contagious! – Week 34. We live in a sea of energies that affects everyone to varying degrees. When two or more are gathered together, there is a collective field that could also be described as a group consciousness or resonance. It is a kind of communal melding of everyone's state of being that generates what we sometimes call "an atmosphere". No doubt this melding includes animals, plants and all else that vibrates in the space, but we will stay with humans for now.

When we enter into a collective field we usually have a sense of how it feels and would no doubt notice a change if someone with a strong personality, powerful emotions or radiating calm entered. When individuals in the field are having diverse thoughts and emotions, a sense of fragmentation can be felt, making it difficult to focus. So, the whole is affected by the vibrational offering of every person, and the dynamics and feel of the group shift accordingly.

HOW THEN CAN WE BE PROACTIVE
IN CREATING A COHERENT GROUP FIELD?

The Findhorn Foundation[76] uses "attunements" and members lead a simple version of the steps on the practice page before most group experiences. Leaders of sports teams do it by focussing the team on positive words, images and feelings of confidence before a game. A good host/facilitator makes sure guests or attendees are clear on the event's purpose and provides opportunity for people to connect early on, which tends to increase feelings of safety and receptivity.

In 2008 I began a massive field-creating venture. It took three years! I designed my eco-home, Heartwood, from a shell of a building with the intention of creating a specific field into which others would come and be positively affected. I stood in the rubble and dedicated it to the good of all who entered. I used lots of wood, including a tree trunk from our land in the spiral staircase, created arched doors that have a sacred feel, and cemented heart-shaped stones into walls. It worked! I was blessed to have this big opportunity, but everyone can do *something* creative to affect the field.

Story Time

A Group Gives Birth

When I was working in the field of birth with my then husband, Abel, we were invited to attend the birth of our dear friend Debbie's first baby – a planned home water birth in our prototype birthing tub. (We later manufactured and hired out birthing tubs as our business.)

When we arrived on the evening that the labour began, I counted nine people present in all – three other friends, Debbie's mother and two midwives, most of whom did not know each other. I sensed a scattered energy: some people were chatting, others busily clattering in the kitchen, while Debbie laboured intensely with one or other birth supporter. There seemed to be no cohesion of purpose and a general nervousness around – especially when we were told by a midwife, "Settle in, this baby will be a long time coming".

Realising that Debbie would be giving birth into our group field, I pulled cushions and seats in the living room into a rough circle and called everyone in – apart from Debbie and one of the midwives who stayed in the birthing room. I voiced that we had chosen to be here to play our part in the welcoming of this baby and then suggested that each person say something about him/herself in relation to being there. During this time of sharing, I sensed a major shift – a new ease and openness with each other was arising.

As we completed the sharing, someone started to sing a simple chant and we all joined in, creating a wonderful sound. It was during this singing that we heard a voice calling from the other room, "You'd better get in here now – we're having a baby!" We were not expecting this at all and sat stunned for a moment, looking at each other. It was clear to me that we all knew that indeed *we* were having the baby. We had become like one body by literally harmonising.

In we went together and calmly gathered around the tub as Debbie started to push. It was an exquisite birth, with baby Ayla gently emerging into the warm water and opening and closing her arms and eyes as some of us wept into the water. Inside I was jubilantly thinking, "we've done it, we've done it!"

* The Practice *

In the Field

Read the steps below, knowing that they will not all apply to every event. You can add to them and use them informally or formally.

Steps to Creating a Cohesive Group Field

♦ **Invite others** (one or more) stating the purpose, place, timing and other details *clearly*. This is the "call" that they will answer… or not.

♦ **Prepare the space** paying attention to lighting, heating, smells, special touches and especially seating. Can people see and hear?

♦ **Welcome each person** so that they feel cared for and "at home".

♦ **Speak out any intentions/desires** for the group and qualities you want to be present, e.g. I am calling for a calm meeting to focus on...

♦ **Connect everyone** in an appropriate way and give each person a chance for their voice to be heard near the beginning – inclusion.

♦ **Engage in the purpose** of the gathering and reach for the best. What will keep the group connected, uplift them and fulfil the task?

♦ **Express gratitude** and maybe summarise what's been experienced.

♦ **Complete together** on time if possible. Feeling complete is important, as is clarity about where the group is headed, if continuing.

Now think of a gathering of two or more you recently hosted or attended and consider whether the appropriate steps above were applied or not and how this affected the group. They can be used for anything from dinner for two, to a party, meeting or sporting activity.

♦ Which steps might be useful to add when you are hosting a gathering or to slip unobtrusively into an event you are at?

During "In the Field" Week

Attune to the group field whenever in company. Test out positively affecting a field by using any of the steps above or any other ideas, e.g.: play music at the start and finish of a meeting to connect attendees; approach those who look the most lost at an event to help them feel more connected; take a bunch of flowers to a meeting.

Discuss with someone anything of interest to you about group fields.

Supportive Resource: Rupert Sheldrake on Morphic Resonance.[77]

WEEK 51

Beyond Separation

Experiencing communion

* Opportunity *

To recognise the illusion of separation and
to experience more communion with others.

*Our perception of solidity
supports the notion that we are separate.
If we could see the moving,
dynamic particles
which form the illusion of matter,
humanity's consciousness
would move mountains in an instant.*

~ CARMELLA B'HAHN
(Paraphrased from *Benjaya's Gifts*[78])

PLEASE NOTE
*If you can't find a partner for this week's exercise,
stay open to finding one soon and do the exercise in the mirror.
Also, look for ways to enter deeper communion with
a young child, animal, lover, friends – as mentioned.*

There is a joke in which a Buddhist goes into a burger bar and says, "Make me one with everything!" This chapter asks how we can taste a way of relating that transcends individuality and leaves us feeling so at one that the sense of "me" and "you" or "it" disappears.

This is the place where we lose ourselves in the ageless wisdom of a newborn's eyes, where we feel inexplicably connected with an animal or blissfully at one with our lover. It is where we are so attuned that we speak each other's thoughts and a kind of transmission is felt. It is where musicians play or sing together and feel united in harmony, and where words – that are dualistic in nature – are inadequate to translate experience. It is what our persona self longs for, without clarity about what we crave. And so we fill the perceived void – the sense of lack – with substitutes like food, screen entertainment, sex, drugs, alcohol or sleep.

Here are three states from which we can relate:
1. The limited personal self/ego that likes to believe it is the be-all and end-all and doesn't want to imagine there could be more.
2. The free, transpersonal witness – sometimes called the "soul" or "Self" – that knows it is not the persona but still has its own flavour.
3. "Unity consciousness" where *everything* is experienced as one – hailed by quantum physics and wisdom traditions alike as the infinite, intelligent energy beyond time and space that is life itself.

IN UNITY CONSCIOUSNESS "I" BECOMES MEANINGLESS
and we can legitimately use "we" statements because we *are* the we.

The work of this course has been primarily about discovering and residing in the second place of soul/Self more so that we can then naturally drop into the third state with others: a state that poet, Mark Nepo, describes as, "the wordless current of being… below the noise of the world". It is from this place that our vision penetrates beyond separate surfaces, allowing us to relate soul to soul.

Paradoxically, the more we do our inner work and learn how to relate from the soul/Self, the more we will experience the merging of the inner and outer and realise that there is, in truth, no separation.

Story Time

Infinite Connections

I had experienced a very difficult ending to a relationship, and while mourning this loss, I noticed that a similar pattern had played itself out in many of my relationships with men. It was, in fact, the exact pattern that my mother was in anguish about when pregnant with me 56 years previously. Had I been carrying this pattern's vibration unconsciously? Could it have passed on to my son? I wanted help to understand and heal this and I trusted that answers would appear if I kept alert.

Within a few days, out of the blue, two people spoke to me on this subject. Firstly, my mother informed me that she had just been told that she needed to work at healing the bloodline and intended find out more about it! Then, at community gardening, I was asked to go and do weeding with Peter Chappell (an elder homeopath). I asked him how his trip to Africa had been, and he said: "I have a story to tell you!" Here it is:

A young mother came to me with her 2½ year old child who didn't walk or talk. She had been very weak with no muscle power since birth. When you lifted an arm or leg and let it go, it just flopped back down. The mother's one younger and two older children were all well, so this wasn't a genetic defect.

I asked her what had happened in the pregnancy and she told me that her husband's brother was murdered by thieves while stealing his motorbike, and she was the first on the scene. In effect, she had been suffering post-traumatic stress disorder for three years – constantly replaying this event. Being something of an expert in how to treat post-traumatic stress, I gave her the trauma one-minute "sound file" to listen to. [79]

Three days later she returned, as I wanted to video any changes. I flipped the girl's legs and arms and realised that they didn't flop any more. The mother told me that her daughter had started walking by clinging onto the table. When asked about the shock that happened in pregnancy she said she couldn't remember it now. So we had treated the mother, and her child started to walk! If this had not been treated it could have imprinted down many generations and any similar trauma would have reactivated it.

On hearing my story, Peter also blessed me with a healing sound, and hopefully that pattern is healed now. I was left deeply moved by a sense of intertwined connection with all the characters above, as well as with an orchestrating intelligence that had provided me with such swift answers.

* The Practice *

Beyond Separation

Humour me, and without questioning why or having to agree with the statements, say slowly and repeatedly for about a minute, "I love myself" and note any inner responses/reactions. Take another minute and state repeatedly, "I am love" and feel your responses/reactions.

Write in your journal about anything arising and then ask yourself:

+ Who is the "I" and who is the "myself" – are they separate?

During "Beyond Separation" Week

You will need a partner for this simple and yet advanced exercise in intimacy, and possibly some courage. Choose carefully who might be up for this and would be willing to join you in a supportive spirit.

Eye Gazing Exercise (To open to a deeper level of communion.)

Preparation: You need – 40 min. uninterrupted space with preceding time for you both to let go of busyness into a calm state; two chairs (or cushions if you want to sit on the floor) opposite each other so that when seated your knees are almost touching; tissues; a clock; a nominated time-keeper.

Read out and then follow these guidelines once seated:

+ Agree to do your best to stay with the eye gazing for at least 20 min.

+ Sink into holding each other's gaze *softly*, concentrating on both eyes, one eye, or a place between and behind the eyes.

+ Keep silent unless it seems necessary to state something.

+ Wait patiently, allowing any awkwardness to simply be there as the mind resists, and relax into *whatever* you feel or see. Laugh, cry freely.

+ Let your gaze penetrate any personality mask to this person's essence and practise accepting them and allowing their acceptance of you.

+ Relax, more and more, observe thoughts, allow feelings and notice how your attention moves from self to other to the greater field.

+ Stop or agree to carry on after 20 min., then share your experiences.

Eye gazing can deepen in further sessions, taking you closer to communion. Decide together whether you want to repeat this experiment a few times to see what unfolds. Discuss the "I Love Myself/Am Love exercise and the concept of separation with others and capture insights in your journal.

Supportive Resource: *Rumi, Gazing at the Beloved* by Will Johnson.[80]

Gratitude's Grace

Living in appreciation

> ### * Opportunity *
>
> To uplift ourselves and nourish our relationships by
> fostering and expressing more appreciation.

*The litmus test for self-realisation
is the constant state
of gratitude.*

~ BYRON KATIE
(Author and Self-awareness Facilitator)

Gratitude emerges as if with grace as a consequence of inner work.

THE MORE IN TOUCH WITH OUR TRUE ESSENCE WE ARE,
THE MORE WE WILL BASK
IN A GENERAL SENSE OF FEELING BLESSED.

When our ego is sleeping, gratitude bubbles up, along with joy. Life's challenges feel more in perspective when we have reduced our conceptualizing, criticizing, categorizing, can express anger with heart and are communicating authentically and with integrity. Appreciation flows when we are embracing what is happening, allowing mistakes and differences, are comfortable with the unknown and have learned how to just be, spaciously.

In other words, when we are perceiving life through the lens of the inside-out paradigm, gratitude is present – no matter what the external circumstance. When perceiving life from the outside-in paradigm, where our judgmental self lives, gratitude can't get a look in… except when life is going just the way we want it to.

Of course, we move in and out of awareness, therefore we will slip into ingratitude and will be lulled into taking familiar things for granted instead of feeling thankful for their existence. So, given this, how can we give gratitude a helping hand and actively foster more appreciation in our daily lives?

As we saw in What *Do* I Want? – Week 38, as long as we are focusing on what we *don't* have or are lacking in ourselves, we will attract more of that into our lives. So the obvious route to gratitude is to focus on what we *do* have. A specific action attached to a regular activity helps to anchor this practice. Here are three examples:

- Before each meal, light a candle and say a few words of gratitude about anything real in the moment – including the food. If and when it feels right, invite others to do likewise.
- Do an "appreciation round" before a meeting to set an uplifting tone – "What I am grateful for about this group/our work is…"
- When you notice anything you like about someone, tell them!

Story Time

With Thanks!
Abigail Robinson

I looked at the consultant and wept. He hadn't listened. Not to the nurses or to me. I hadn't yet been able to stand up alone without blacking out. I would then pick myself up and manage to be upright in short bursts, but I was afraid to go home and be alone there. I had no money and there was no public transport; it was Easter Sunday. He had no idea what was wrong with me, but they didn't have enough staff working to do the tests and he was clearing beds. Ruthlessly and coldly he told me that whatever was wrong with me, it would probably be there for the rest of my life.

I felt a sense of cold fire and kept seeing myself in a police cell for murdering this man. I felt nothing but a sense of satisfaction at brutally dispatching him. It frightened me that I had no fear... I did not want to be someone like this. I didn't want to play God, like him.

I decided the only antidote was gratitude. Whatever else was wrong with me, I did know it would not be good to walk out of that hospital filled with such hate. I felt an urge to thank every person who had showed me any decency, any kindness, any humanity and to let them know the impact it had made. It felt really important to be clear that a smile had lifted my day.

Every cleaner who had shown me a smile or said good morning was thanked, as was the health care assistant who had made me two cups of tea when I had been without water in the waiting room for 13 hours. I thanked the main nurse who had taken care of me and insisted I did not try standing up without help. She cried while I hugged her and she told me there was something really wrong and to hassle my GP until they helped me. I thanked another nurse who advised me not to take the consultant personally, that he treated everyone like that, including the staff.

As I thanked each person, I felt my dignity and humanity being restored to me, piece by piece. I felt their care again, as well as *their* gratitude on hearing mine; and so gratitude continued building billowing waves of kindness, warmth and tears.

* The Practice *

Gratitude's Grace

On this last week, read the Paradigms of Relating model again and revisit where you stood when you started this course. Then appraise where you are now, focussing on what has moved in you. Write in your journal about anything that feels important.

Next, take a sweeping overview of the way you now relate to yourself, others and life and summarise, as best you can, your overall level of gratitude and how much appreciation you feel and express.

During "Gratitude's Grace" Week

1. Discuss with someone – a partner or group if you have one – how you see yourself now in relation to the two paradigms and whether your appreciation levels have increased since starting the course.

2. Implement regular activities (reread the three examples for ideas).

3. Choose a relationship in which you would like to cultivate more gratitude and see how many *genuine* appreciations you can give this week.

Researchers tell us that successful relationships depend on mutual appreciation, which acts as a safe harbour when weathering disagreements, but expressing appreciation in a way that touches someone deeply is a skill. Remember "I" statements (Week 9). Being specific and using "I" statements rather than unspecific "you" statements will make the world of difference, for example:

> **Unspecific "you" statement:** You were wonderful tonight!
> (Begs questions such as: "In what way?" or "How did it affect you?")

> **Specific "I" statement:** When you spoke confidently tonight, I was delighted because I know how far you have come this year.

If you have been sharing *Heart of Relating* with others, share your gratitude for your time together and plan a completion party/dinner.

Supportive Resource: *Gratitude*: Louie Schwartzberg (short video).[81]

* I deeply appreciate *

- You for relating with my lifelong work and making it more worthwhile.

- The many teachers from whom I have absorbed what I know – whether in person or otherwise – including: my parents, Paul Solomon, John Seymour (NLP), Marshall Rosenberg (NVC), Eckhart Tolle, Richard Moss, Caroline Myss, Byron Katie, Abraham-Hicks.

- All those whose stories and wisdom I have used in this book.

- My soul-friend, Linda Lantieri, for being inspiring, always believing in me and supporting my offerings to the world.

- My lovely proofreaders Sally Eaves and Katie Fretwell, and everyone who has given truthful feedback on various manuscripts.

- All members of the first *Heart of Relating* group on whom I piloted the course for the good of those following in their footsteps.

- Those who have generously supported this project financially.

- Members of the Bowden House Community and my son, Asher, who have presented me with an excellent training ground in living the skills I have presented.

- Matador/Troubador Publishers, Helen Lewis at Literally PR, and all who helped this course find its readers/participants.

Words do not teach at all.
It is life experience that brings you your knowing.
But when you hear words that are a vibrational match
to the knowing that you have accumulated,
then sometimes it's easier
for you to sort it all out.

~ ABRAHAM-HICKS
(Wisdom Teachers)

Life spirals us round and through the same lessons in life,
each time with the opportunity to live our understanding more fully.
If you dare to return to beginning of *Heart of Relating*
to run through the whole cycle again,
you might be astounded by how much more sense it all makes
now that you have the fuller perspective
of this hologram of relating from the heart of who you are.

There is no end to education.
It is not that you read a book,
pass an examination,
and finish with education.
The whole of life,
from the moment you are born
to the moment you die,
is a process of learning.

~ KRISHNAMURTI
(Speaker, Writer and Sage)

Guide to Using Heart of Relating

Solo (Option A)

Prioritise a 45-minute timeslot that you can commit to *at the same time* every week – a sacrosanct space where you can focus. Having it in your diary as part of your weekly rhythm will help you keep to it. This matters because the later you leave reading what you need to do during the week, the less time you have to engage with and observe live examples of that aspect of relating in action. Sometimes you will need less than 45 minutes and sometimes a little more.

WEEK 1
In your first 45-minute slot: Reread all the introductory pages as there is a lot to take in on one reading. Then read the first week's lesson and do the exercise and journal work from the practice page.

During the rest of the week: Complete the suggestions under the heading, During "Awakening the Body" Week. Continue to make notes in your journal and talk freely about the theme with others.

WEEK 2 – 52
In your 45-minute slot: Review any learning from the previous week for the first 10 minutes or so, and answer:

What has had impact and how will I choose to apply this in my life?

Then read the next section thoroughly, preferably more than once, (things usually sink in deeper on subsequent readings) and complete any suggested journal work or exercises.

During each week
Apply the practice suggestions and, as often as you can, discuss the theme and involve others informally as you go along. This helps expand understanding and integrate the lessons – especially for those who learn better through interaction. If others witness you doing this work it will probably support you to carry on. Hopefully they will want to join in. Catch all insights in your journal.

Duo or Study Group (Option B)

A twosome or group is *strongly recommended* because:
- This will give you the perfect opportunity to improve your relationship with your partner/friend or group.
- Sharing insights, being supported and witnessed can keep you on track and make sure you stay the course.
- Hearing the experience of others will expand your knowledge and understanding of the subject.
- Transforming habit patterns can be thrilling and freeing, and is worth celebrating with others.

Your partner, family, friends, workmates could be ideal in your duo/ group and it is worth being patient until you find a combination you feel happy with. Each person will need a copy of the book unless you are in the same home and can manage to share.

The journal work and weekly practice will be done alone, although on-going discussion about the theme with others during the week is encouraged. Then you will be sharing and expanding your learning in a focussed way in your duo/group *at the end* of each practice week.

Steps in the duo/group process
- Find a partner or group and agree on a weekly meeting time.
(Take your time – this decision will affect participants deeply.)
- Use your first meeting to connect, get clear on the process and decide on group agreements – see following suggested format.
- Soon after (the next day if possible), take 45 minutes alone to complete the first section's exercise/journal work.
- During the week, apply all the practice suggestions.
- Meet again after one week to review your learning together.
- Within 24 hours, begin the following week's lesson. (Again, the longer you leave it, the less time you have to practise.)

Suggested length of meetings
One hour minimum for a duo; one and a half hours for three to five; two hours for six plus. (If your group is over six people, you might want to share in pairs before feeding back to the larger group.)

Suggested Format for the FIRST *HR* Duo/Group Meeting

(Before you begin the weekly lessons)

Be prepared! Reread all the introductory pages and the Week 1 section *before* the meeting.

If possible, agree before you meet, which person will keep an eye on timing and focus. Groups usually function better with a facilitator. Sitting roughly in a circle also helps dynamics.

Important: Build in 10/15 minutes social/arrival time before actually starting, then start on time.

1. Time keeper/group facilitator states the purpose of the gathering: *To prepare the ground for this shared adventure in improving our relating and communication skills.*

2. Take a moment's quiet to become more present and to release any distracting thoughts or feelings. Light a candle if it helps you to focus on a different level of sharing.

3. Have a *one minute* "check-in" each to share whether there is still anything that is taking your attention away from being fully present.

4. Next, each speak for a few minutes on a) why you are drawn to focus on your relating skills right now and b) anything you want others to know about your relationship with yourself, others or life.

5. Now make some agreements about what would help you feel safe in these meetings and to stay on track, and write them down, e.g.:
  • Listen, allowing each to speak without interruption
  • Make sure everyone's voice is heard
  • Avoid giving unsolicited advice or "fixing" each other
  • Keep what each person says confidential.

6. Make sure you are each clear about what you are agreeing to – see Suggested Format for 2-52, and then have an open space to voice anything else such as worries or timing concerns. End on time with a quiet moment and maybe blowing out the candle together if there is one.

Suggested Format for *HR* Duo/Group Meetings 2-52

Time keeper/facilitator to check in advance whether a practice page exercise may be beneficial to do together – there are a few.

Minimise distractions, e.g. phones, others in and out of the space.

1. Take a minute's silence to "land" together in the space – lighting a candle to invite a shift to a deeper level of sharing if you like. At the end of the silence, have one person state the specific topic of the week and read aloud that week's opportunity and quote.

2. A *quick* check-in for each person to air anything they are experiencing *in the moment* that might affect their full presence during this time, e.g. "I am distracted by a headache".

3. In turn, take *uninterrupted* space to share what you have learned during the week – about 5 minutes each. This will help practise deep listening. Refer to the practice page and your journal.

4. Occasionally, complete an exercise together and share your results. Set a time limit for this and keep on track.

5. Open sharing-time about the current topic. Remember that you don't need instant answers to questions raised or to fix anything or anyone. Open to continual enquiry and catch insights in your journal.

6. Each answer succinctly, *What has had impact this week and how will I choose to apply this in my life?*

7. Read in silence together the coming week's topic so that you know where you are headed next. Seek clarity from each other if you don't understand anything or just trust and do your best.

8. End with a short silence and blow out the candle if you have one.

If you have to miss a meeting, let others know in good time and keep up with Skype or a phone call with one member of the group.

Near the end of the course, check whether members want to continue in some form; begin again? Do you want to plan a completion celebration?

Possibly the most effective
communication tool
is a heartfelt smile ☺

About the Author

Carmella B'Hahn was born in the Midlands of England in 1958.

She has had a fascination since childhood with the subject of relating and communication, having suffered a mysterious fear of speaking that took thirty years to dissolve.

She has completed many trainings, but life itself – particularly birth and death – has been her greatest teacher. The sudden death of her first son, aged five, and subsequent miscarriages taught her the importance of living from her inner strength, and now she assists others to do likewise. Presently this takes the form of communications coaching, grief counselling and courses supported by the teachings from her three books, *Heart of Relating*, *Mourning Has Broken* and *Benjaya's Gifts*.

Carmella co-founded: *MetaCentre: Foundation for Human Potential* in 1984; *BirthWorks* (now franchised) in 1987, which offers support services for holistic birth and waterbirth; and *The Transitus Network* (www.martinsey.org.uk) in 2004, which honours the sacred process of living and dying.

Since 2002, Carmella has been on the team of *The Inner Resilience Program* in New York City, founded and directed by Linda Lantieri, which supports school personnel to connect with their inner lives (www.innerresilience-tidescenter.org).

In 2005 she co-created her ideal living conditions – an intentional eco-community called Bowden House Community in Totnes, Devon, UK. Given the 33 adults and 14 children who co-habit this land with her, it has become her playground for practising and learning a multitude of relating skills.

Carmella's website is www.heartofrelating.com

Endnotes

Citations and Supportive Resources

[1] The "Conscious Competence" learning model was adapted by Carmella B'Hahn with input from Collette Lyons. It's origin is thought to be an oriental proverb – "He Who Knows Not". One version is from Gordon Training International in the early 1970s. Full article on the model see: www.businessballs.com/consciouscompetencelearningmodel.htm

[2] Abigail Robinson's website: www.sacred-sound.co.uk

[3] David Abram's teachings: www.wildethics.org
David Abram clip: www.youtube.com/watch?v=2IGdzAt_dwI

[4] Thomas Huebl's teachings: www.thomashuebl.com

[5] Sir Ken Robinson, *How Schools Kill Creativity* video, TED2006: www.ted.com/talks/ken_robinson_says_schools_kill_creativity.html

[6] Carmella and M'haletta B'Hahn, *Benjaya's Gifts*, Hazelwood Press, 1996, p.57. www.heartofrelating.com

[7] Anita Moorjani, *Dying to be Me*, Hay House, 2012, p.69.

[8] Ken Wilber, *The Pocket Ken Wilber*, Shambhala Publications Inc., 2008, p.2-3. These statements are a variant of the original disidentification exercises of Dr Roberto Assagioli, founder of Psychosynthesis.

[9] Richard Moss, *Inside-Out Healing*, Hay House, 2011. www.richardmoss.com

[10] Eckhart Tolle, *A New Earth*, Penguin Books, 2005. www.eckharttolle.com

[11] Dr Wayne W. Dyer, *Pulling Your Own Strings,* Hamlyn Books, 1979. (A psychological classic, still in print with Arrow Books.)

[12] Dr Robin Stern, *The Gaslight Effect,* Morgan Road Books, 2007. (For those feeling seriously victimised in a controlling relationship.)

[13] Carmella B'Hahn, *Mourning Has Broken,* Crucible Publishers, 2002, p.100. www.heartofrelating.com

[14] Miles Sherts, *Conscious Communication,* Langdon Street Press, 2009.

[15] Malcolm Stern and Sujata Bristow, *The Courage to Love,* Piatkus, 1996.

[16] The Sacred Art of Listening: www.sacredlistening.com

[17] Marshall Rosenberg founded *The Center for Nonviolent Communication* (international) www.cnvc.org. Also see www.nvc-uk.com (UK).

[18] According to the online encyclopedia, Wikipedia, many e-mail messages like this circulated in 2003, which were started by a letter to the *New Scientist* magazine from Graham Rawlinson of Nottingham University in which he discusses his Ph. D thesis. There is much more to the science of word recognition but this simple example makes a point.

[19] Wayne Muller, *Sabbath, Restoring the Sacred Rhythm of Rest*, Bantam Books, 1999.

[20] A Cherokee Tale, adapted from *Poetry for the Journey* www.davidstanleybell.com/poetry/index.htm

[21] Nancy Carlsson-Paige, *Taking Back Childhood, Helping children thrive in a fast-paced, media-saturated world*, Hudson Street Press, 2008.

[22] *Positive News* reports on positive developments from across the world, helping to create a more constructive media. www.positivenews.org.uk

[23] Carmella and M'haletta B'Hahn, *Benjaya's Gifts*, Hazelwood Press, 1996. www.heartofrelating.com

[24] Jon Kabat-Zinn: en.wikipedia.org/iki/Jon_Kabat-Zinn

[25] Caroline Myss, *Energy Anatomy* CD set, Sounds True, 1996.

[26] Sharon Maas, *Of Marriageable Age*, Bookouture, 2014.

[27] Kelly Bryson, New Culture Community and NVC Principles. 15 min YouTube clip: www.youtube.com/watch?v=0r86bd3oYHE

[28] Kelly Bryson, *Don't Be Nice, Be Real*, Elite Books, 2004. languageofcompassion.com/resources/books-videos-and-cds/

[29] Research on the human heart see: www.heartmath.org.

[30] Jay C., Brain – Left or Right (a clear article about our brain functioning): www.buzzle.com/editorials/9-27-2004-59837.asp

[31] Spinning Lady test to see if you are right or left brain dominant: www.illumine.co.uk/resources/brain-fitness/spinning-lady.html

[32] Rosalie Gerut: www.rosaliegerut.com and www.one-by-one.org

[33] Carmella B'Hahn, *Mourning Has Broken*, Crucible Publishers, 2002, full story p.147-158. www.heartofrelating.com

[34] Created by Carmella B'Hahn. Inspired by various therapies.

[35] Peter Elbow, The Believing Game and How to Make Conflicting Opinions More Fruitful. From the book: *Nurturing the Peacemakers in Our Students: A Guide to Teaching Peace, Empathy and Understanding*, 2006, edited by Chris Weber. works.bepress.com/peter_elbow/10

36 Joan Tollifson, *Awake in the Heartland, The Ecstasy of What Is,* Non-Duality Press, 2011, p.32.

37 Eckhart Tolle, *A New Earth*, Penguin Books, 2005, p.137.

38 See *A New Earth* (above) for a chapter on the "Pain Body" and emotions, p.129.

39 Dr Richard Moss, *Inside-Out Healing,* Hay House, 2011, p.139-147. www.richardmoss.com

40 Whole story in *Benjaya's Gifts* by Carmella and M'haletta B'Hahn, Hazelwood Press, 1996. www.heartofrelating.com

41 Neuro Linguistic Programming (NLP). Roger Ellerton, Perceptual Positions: www.renewal.ca/nlp16.htm

42 Abraham-Hicks, excerpt from a workshop in San Rafael, CA, 1999. www.abrahamhicks.com

43 Kevin B. Wright and Lynne M. Webb, *Computer-Mediated Communication in Personal Relationships*, Peter Lang Publishing, 2011.

44 Carmella and M'haletta B'Hahn, *Benjaya's Gifts*, Hazelwood Press, 1996. www.heartofrelating.com

45 Joseph M. Marshall III, *Walking With Grandfather, The Wisdom of Lakota Elders,* Sounds True, 2005.

46 Giacomo Rizzolatti, an interview excerpt quoted in Sandra Blakeslee, "Cells that read Minds." *New York Times,* Jan 10th, 2006. www.nytimes.com/2006/01/10/science/10mirr.html

47 Daniel Goleman, *Social Intelligence*, Arrow Books, 2007.

48 Girl Scouts website: forgirls.girlscouts.org/end-bullying-by-speaking-out

49 More ideas about needs in Abraham Maslow's Hierarchy of Needs theory proposed in his 1943 paper "A Theory of Human Motivation" in *Psychological Review.* en.wikipedia.org/wiki/Maslow's_hierarchy_of_needs

50 Byron Katie, *Question Your Thinking, Change the World,* Hay House, 2007, p.2.

51 Byron Katie, *I Need Your Love - Is That True?* Three Rivers Press, 2005.

52 Marshall B. Rosenberg, *Nonviolent Communication: A Language of Life*, PuddleDancer Press, 2003, p.52.

53 Doreen Virtue and Grant Virtue, *Angel Words*, Hay House, 2010. www.amazon.com/dp/1401926967/ref=tsm_1_fb_lk

54 Doreen Virtue, Facebook blog, June 2013: www.facebook.com/DoreenVirtue444/posts/557039337670715

55 Neuro Linguistic Programming (NLP) teaches in-depth methods for creating outcomes: www.exforsys.com/tutorials/nlp/nlp-well-formed-outcome-model.html

56 Robert Augustus Masters, *Emotional Intimacy*, Sounds True, 2013.

57 Taken from the Prologue of *Social Intelligence*, Daniel Goleman. The Soldiers at the Mosque were reported on *All Things Considered*, National Public Radio (USA), April 4th, 2003.

58 Miles Sherts, *Conscious Communication*, Langdon Street Press, 2009.

59 John Gray, *Men Are From Mars, Women Are From Venus*, Thorsons, 1993.

60 Mark Nepo, *Seven Thousand Ways to Listen*, Free Press, 2012, p.50.

61 Obviously, all levels of conflict are not normal. Professional help will need to be sought when intense conflict, especially including physical violence, is occurring.

62 Douglas Stone, Bruce Patton and Sheila Heen, *Difficult Conversations*, Viking Penguin, 1999.

63 Malcolm Stern and Sujata Bristow, *The Courage To Love*, Piatkus, 1996.

64 An NLP (Neuro Linguistic Programming) definition. Google "reframing" for further information.

65 If you need extra support it is suggested that you read Colin Tipping's book, *Radical Forgiveness* (see below), and seek help from a psychotherapist if need be.

66 Carmella B'Hahn, *Mourning Has Broken*, Crucible Publishers, 2002, Arun Gandhi's story p.141. www.heartofrelating.com

67 Colin C. Tipping, *Radical Forgiveness*, Gateway, 2000.

68 From the online encyclopedia, Wikipedia.

69 Eric E. Vogt, Juanita Brown, and David Isaacs, *The Art of Powerful Questions, Catalyzing Insight, Innovation, and Action*. September 2003. Published by Whole Systems Associates, CA, USA.
www.cihm.leeds.ac.uk/document_downloads/Art_of_Powerful_Questions.pdf

70 Richard Bach, *Illusions, The Adventures of a Reluctant Messiah*, Pan Books, 1977.

71 Ken Robinson, TED2006. This story is also told in Ken Robinson's book, *The Element*, Penguin Books, 2009.

72 Rescuer/victim/persecutor are common co-dependent roles about which much has been written. Google for more information.

73 Kahlil Gibran, *The Madman: His Parables and Poems* available as a free ebook online at www.gutenberg.org. Also published by Penguin, Random House, Canada, 2011.

74 Eckhart Tolle, *The New Earth*, Penguin Books, 2005, p.104.

75 An excerpt from Dr Brokenleg's article, Transforming Cultural Trauma into Resilience, Fall 2012 issue of *Reclaiming Children and Youth*.

76 The Findhorn Foundation is a large, intentional spiritual community, education centre and ecovillage in Scotland.

77 Rupert Sheldrake, *Morphic Resonance: The Nature of Formative Causation,* Park Street Press, 2009. www.sheldrake.org

78 Carmella and M'haletta B'Hahn, *Benjaya's Gifts*, Hazelwood Press, 1996, p 238. www.heartofrelating.com

79 See more about Peter Chappell's sound healing: www.detox.zone

80 Will Johnson, *Rumi, Gazing at the Beloved. The Radical Practice of Beholding the Divine.* Inner Traditions International, Rochester, Vermont, 2003.

81 A moving short film on Gratitude, starting at 3.45 minutes into Louie Schwartzberg's TEDxSF talk: www.youtube.com/watch?v=gXDMoiEkyuQ